Building Assets Is Elementary

Group Activities for Helping Kids Ages 8-12 Succeed

Search INSTITUTE

Practical research benefiting children and youth

Building Assets Is Elementary:
Group Activities for Helping Kids Ages 8–12 Succeed

At the time of publication, all facts and figures cited herein are the most current available; all telephone numbers, addresses, and Web site URLs are accurate and active; all publications, organizations, Web sites, and other resources exist as described in this book; and all efforts have been made to verify them. The author and Search Institute make no warranty or guarantee concerning the information and materials given out by organizations or content found at Web sites that are cited herein, and we are not responsible for any changes that occur after this book's publication. If you find an error or believe that a resource listed herein is not as described, please contact Client Services at Search Institute.

About Search Institute
Search Institute is an independent, nonprofit, nonsectarian organization whose mission is to provide leadership, knowledge, and resources to promote healthy children, youth, and communities. The institute collaborates with others to promote long-term organizational and cultural change that supports its mission. For a free information packet, call 800-888-7828.

Search Institute
615 First Avenue Northeast, Suite 125
Minneapolis, MN 55413
www.search-institute.org
612-376-8955 • 800-888-7828

ISBN: 1-57482-836-3

Library of Congress Cataloging-in-Publication Data

Welch, Rita.
  Building assets is elementary : group activities for helping kids ages 8-12 succeed / Rita Welch, Tenessa Gemelke.
    p. cm.
  ISBN 1-57482-836-3
Children—Conduct of life. 2. Children—Life skills guides.
I. Gemelke, Tenessa, 1975- II. Title.
BJ1631 .W45 2004
305.234—dc22
                    2003026523

Credits
Contributing Writers: Rita Welch, Tenessa Gemelke
Editors: Ruth Taswell, Tenessa Gemelke, Jacqueline White
Design: Nancy Johansen-Wester

Licensing and Copyright

Printing Tips
To produce high-quality copies of activity sheets for distribution without spending a lot of money, follow these tips:

- Always copy from the original. Copying from a copy lowers the reproduction quality.

- Make copies more appealing by using brightly colored paper or colored ink. Quick-print shops often run daily specials on certain colors of ink.

- For variety, consider printing each activity sheet on a different color of paper.

- If you are using more than one activity sheet or an activity sheet that runs more than one page, make two-sided copies.

- Make sure the paper weight is heavy enough (use at least 60-pound offset paper) so that the words don't bleed through (e.g., as often happens with 20-pound paper).

Contents

Introduction
Life Packs for Success

How does a 9-year-old learn to negotiate with her parents for permission to ride her bike alone to a city park? What helps an 11-year-old know what to do when he sees someone sitting without any friends during lunchtime? What information and experience does a 10-year-old need in order to choose a healthy snack over candy?

Children ages 8 to 12 are beginning to "come into their own," recognizing how best to handle more and more of the situations life presents, but they still have a lot to learn. As adults, we can help them by providing the tools, skills, knowledge, and experiences that they need to be increasingly independent.

Just as we work with children to make sure their backpacks are filled with vital school supplies or gear for out-of-school time activities, we must also work together to fill each child's "life pack." All adults—parents, teachers, youth leaders, neighbors, extended family, and more—can help give each child the qualities, values, and opportunities he or she will need to do things like negotiate rules, resolve conflicts, act kindly, and make healthy living choices. At Search Institute, we call these vital "life supplies" developmental assets.

The Developmental Assets
The activities and activity sheets in this book are designed to give children tangible opportunities to explore topics relevant to their middle childhood years, while also helping them build developmental assets that will last a lifetime. Whether you're a youth-serving organization leader or a classroom teacher, you can use these activities as invitations to learning—they'll help you help your group of kids try new strategies, connect with others, and see how to apply age-appropriate asset-building skills in real-world, everyday situations.

Search Institute's surveys of more than 200,000 young people show that the developmental assets are powerful and important influences on youth behavior. The more developmental assets a young person reports, the less likely he or she is to make harmful or unhealthy choices. Search Institute has now reframed the 40 developmental assets specific to the needs of middle childhood, in addi-

tion to its original list of 40 key developmental assets specific to the needs of adolescents. For the developmental assets framework for middle childhood, see page 9. For more information about the developmental assets in middle childhood, see Search Institute's book *Coming into Their Own: How Developmental Assets Promote Positive Growth in Middle Childhood* by Peter C. Scales, Ph.D., Arturo Sesma, Ph.D., and Brent Bolstrom.

Who This Book Is For
While this book focuses on activities for use with children in grades 4 through 6, keep in mind that a wide range of developmental differences characterizes middle childhood. Some children in grade 4 may still be happy to play with younger children, while also insisting on their own maturity and independence. Some young people in grade 6 retain childlike thoughts and behaviors, while others are well on their way to adolescence and demonstrating greater independence and maturity. "It is in middle childhood," write the authors of *Coming into Their Own,*

> that the first murmurs of the coming early adolescence begin to be heard and the first hints of the transition become apparent. Many children, though still clearly children, begin to occasionally act and feel in ways more characteristic of adolescents. Middle childhood is a time of great change, of enormous expansion of children's worlds and understandings of self and others, and a time when children's self-structures, values, beliefs, and aspirations are still malleable and relatively optimistic.

As children in grades 4 through 6 grow, they often struggle between needing more choices, higher personal control, and greater independence and not necessarily having all the skills to readily manage their expanding world. Such struggles often engage parents, teachers, coaches, and other adults in challenges over homework, bedtime, and other limit issues.

You have an opportunity to help ease such struggles and engage in positive interactions as a group leader or teacher in a child's life. In whatever context you're using the activities in this book, you are sharing in the responsibility for a child's development. As Scales, Sesma, and Bolstrom point out in *Coming into Their Own*:

> *Children's risks and opportunities both increase in* [middle childhood], *and the changing landscape of risks, opportunities, and emerging capacities can lead either to developmental success or frustration, both in children's present and future. . . . understanding the positive developmental experiences children need during middle childhood is critical for ensuring their well-being. Understanding what children need, and the individual, organizational, and community actions that emerge from that knowledge, can contribute to reducing children's risk behaviors, promoting their resilience, and enhancing their thriving during the upper elementary years, and to enabling them to effectively navigate the gradual transition between childhood and adolescence.*

Feel free to adapt the activities in this book to best suit the unique needs of your particular group of children. For mature preteens, adolescents, and young adults, you can find more advanced asset-building activities in Search Institute's *Building Assets Together: 135 Group Activities for Helping Youth Succeed* and *More Building Assets Together: 130 Activities for Helping Youth Succeed.*

Tips for Working with Groups

Whether you have worked with children for years or are just getting started, keep the following tips in mind:

- Learn the names of all participants and call them by name. This shows that you care about them and are paying attention.
- Instead of declaring your own rules, ask group members to develop and adhere to appropriate ground rules for behavior. Post the rules where all can see them.
- When you give feedback, be sure that you do so in an accepting, respectful, and helpful manner.
- Learn from the children in your group. As you share knowledge and information, invite group members to contribute their own experiences and understanding.
- Let group members struggle with difficult ideas. Instead of intervening and redirecting them immediately, give children some time to explore concepts and search for their own solutions.

Build a Community of Learners

One of a leader's greatest joys in working with a group of children comes from helping them become a community of learners who support and encourage each other's efforts and achievements. As you try the different group activities in this book, aim to bring your kids together as a team. To take the risks necessary for learning and enjoying their learning, kids need to feel safe and accepted in the group.

As the group leader, you have the ability to create the environment in which they can feel safe and accepted. Work side by side with your group of kids. Let them know you are their co-learner. Investigate concepts and practice skill building using the developmental assets mindset together.

The activities and activity sheets in this book are not meant as prescriptive recipes that follow a rigid sequence of instructions. Rather, dig in to the book to find those that work best for your particular group of learners. Use the activities to help children build assets, empowering them to learn what it means to make positive choices that will help them pursue their dreams with confidence and aim to be their best selves.

Be an Asset Builder

As you'll see when you try out the activities in this book, intentionally building assets for and with young people does not require costly programs or an elaborate curriculum. Keep these six asset-building principles in mind, and you'll be well on your way to nurturing assets in all your interactions with young people:

1. **Everyone can build assets.** Youth-serving professionals and teachers are not the only ones who can help build assets—so can parents and guardians, neighbors, coaches, employers, friends, and many others. (For more about being an asset builder, see "What Is an Asset Builder?" on page 7.)
2. **All young people need assets.** While it is crucial to pay special attention to youth who struggle—economically, emotionally, or otherwise—nearly all young people need more assets than they have.
3. **Relationships are key.** Strong relationships between adults and young people, young people and their peers, and teenagers and children are central to asset building.
4. **Asset building is an ongoing process.** Building assets starts when a child is born and continues throughout high school and beyond.
5. **Consistent messages are important.** It is important for families, schools, communities, the media,

What Is an Asset Builder?

While anyone can be an asset builder by beginning with the strengths they already have (or that they develop), specific qualities are characteristic of successful asset builders. Who you *are* is just as important as what you *do* to help build assets with and for the young people you lead in these activities.

Who You Are—"Being" Characteristics
- Open, honest, and an active listener.
- Committed to maintaining integrity, being responsible, and promoting positive change in the world.
- Hopeful and optimistic about young people and the future.
- Appreciative of others' strengths and uniqueness.
- Striving toward caring, respectful relationships with young people.
- Willing to share your "assets" (time, knowledge, caring, experience, wisdom) with young people.

What You Do—"Doing" Characteristics
- Respect and affirm children, seek to understand them, and expect respect in return.
- Look for the good in others and seek common ground with them.
- Hold meaningful conversations with young people about personal values, beliefs, decision making, and cultural differences.
- Model positive behaviors, including kindness, lifelong learning, voting, and self-restraint.
- Forgive people when they make mistakes.
- Know how to apologize, explain, negotiate, and resolve conflicts peacefully.
- Encourage young people to succeed in school, serve their community, and be valuable resources to others.

"Being" and "doing" characteristics adapted from *Essentials of Asset Building: A Curriculum for Trainers—Everyone's an Asset Builder.* Copyright © 2002 by Search Institute; 800-888-7828; www.search-institute.org.

---

and others to all give young people consistent and similar messages about what is important and what is expected of them.

6. **Intentional repetition is important.** Assets must be continually reinforced across the years and in all areas of a young person's life.

How This Book Is Organized

Each chapter of this book contains activities and activity sheets to help you build developmental assets with groups of young people. Chapter 1 focuses on the general concept of the developmental assets; Chapter 2 provides activities to build a positive group dynamic. Subsequent chapters deal with each of the eight asset categories into which the 40 developmental assets for middle childhood are organized.

A brief introduction at the beginning of each chapter gives group leaders a better understanding of the particular asset category. The activities and activity sheets within each chapter provide for a deeper exploration of individual assets. Every activity begins with a "Focus" and "Materials" list. Occasionally, to simplify an activity, we've included a section entitled "Advance Preparations," which indicates a few steps the group leader

may want to take before beginning the activity with the kids. The "Activity" description follows, and is often accompanied by an "Optional Variation" and an activity sheet.

Although the activities are numbered, you need not conduct the activities in any particular order. Focus on the areas that best address the needs of your group. The diverse content of the activities also addresses multiple learning styles and skill levels, so you can choose the ideas that best reflect your group's abilities.

Ways to Use This Book

You can complete most of the activities in one half-hour meeting, though you can use many as ongoing projects. A few activities involve a follow-up session for reflection. *Because many of the activities would benefit from multiple sessions or advance preparation, be sure to read through the entire activity in advance.*

All of the activities are flexible so that you can use them in a variety of combinations and formats. Some of the activities include optional variations, but feel free to create your own adaptations. Here are a few possibilities:
- Use a chapter of activities to focus on one asset category.

- Choose individual activities that complement the work that you are already doing with young people.
- Combine several activities to focus on one area of life, such as family or school.
- Invite parents, guardians, or caregivers, as well as older or younger siblings or groups of kids, to participate in activities with your group.
- Use activities sequentially to systematically introduce the eight asset categories.
- Use role playing. (See "Tips for Role Playing" below.)
- Make copies of the "A Pack Full of Assets" Activity Sheet (on page 15) on colored paper to use as a cover for (or to glue or staple on top of a folder)

compiling other completed activity sheets. Give the folders to the group at each gathering, and keep in a safe place for an end-of-the year asset reflection or celebration.

Whether you work in a school, neighborhood, congregation, or any other youth-serving group, these fresh activity ideas will reenergize your efforts and help you build in young people the developmental assets that every young person deserves. *Building Assets Is Elementary* is for all adults who want to help children in middle childhood develop skills that lead to healthy decision making now and in the future.

Tips for Role Playing

Dramatic role playing is a great way to give kids the opportunity to put ideas into practice. Some of the activities in this book encourage role playing. As you invite your group of children to practice new skills in the guise of different characters, you may find these suggestions helpful:

- **Start with something simple.** Build confidence with straightforward situations and gradually add more challenging scenarios for characters to act out.
- **Use familiar and relevant examples.** You may have to modify situations and characters to suit your group's unique experiences and needs. The capabilities of children in grade 4 can differ greatly from those in grade 6. Ask your group to role-play the people, places, and circumstances that are most meaningful to them.
- **Don't embarrass participants.** Give them time to think and rehearse before they demonstrate in front of

the entire group. Small groups performing first for one another may be helpful before appearing in front of the larger group. Coach kids as they rehearse and offer cues and encouragement while they perform. Afterward, ask group members to describe the positive ways that actors showed confidence or strength in challenging situations.

- **Involve everyone.** Invite different kids to demonstrate each time, and invite all participants to role-play in small groups. Be sure to visit each small group to offer your attention and answer questions.
- **Give useful feedback.** Participants are much more likely to use skills in real-world situations if they receive effective feedback. Ask the group to discuss ways to apply their skills at home, at school, and among their friends.

40 Developmental Assets
for Middle Childhood

Search Institute has identified the following building blocks of healthy development that help children grow up healthy, caring, and responsible.

External Assets

SUPPORT

1. **Family support**—Family life provides high levels of love and support.
2. **Positive family communication**—Parent(s) and child communicate positively. Child feels comfortable seeking advice and counsel from parent(s).
3. **Other adult relationships**—Child receives support from adults other than her or his parent(s).
4. **Caring neighborhood**—Child experiences caring neighbors.
5. **Caring school climate**—Relationships with teachers and peers provide a caring, encouraging school environment.
6. **Parent involvement in schooling**—Parent(s) are actively involved in helping the child succeed in school.

EMPOWERMENT

7. **Community values children**—Child feels valued and appreciated by adults in the community.
8. **Children as resources**—Child is included in decisions at home and in the community.
9. **Service to others**—Child has opportunities to help others in the community.
10. **Safety**—Child feels safe at home, at school, and in her or his neighborhood.

BOUNDARIES AND EXPECTATIONS

11. **Family boundaries**—Family has clear and consistent rules and consequences and monitors the child's whereabouts.
12. **School boundaries**—School provides clear rules and consequences.
13. **Neighborhood boundaries**—Neighbors take responsibility for monitoring the child's behavior.
14. **Adult role models**—Parent(s) and other adults in the child's family, as well as nonfamily adults, model positive, responsible behavior.
15. **Positive peer influence**—Child's closest friends model positive, responsible behavior.
16. **High expectations**—Parent(s) and teachers expect the child to do her or his best at school and in other activities.

CONSTRUCTIVE USE OF TIME

17. **Creative activities**—Child participates in music, art, drama, or creative writing two or more times per week.
18. **Child programs**—Child participates two or more times per week in cocurricular school activities or structured community programs for children.
19. **Religious community**—Child attends religious programs or services one or more times per week.
20. **Time at home**—Child spends some time most days both in high-quality interaction with parents and doing things at home other than watching TV or playing video games.

Internal Assets

COMMITMENT TO LEARNING

21. **Achievement motivation**—Child is motivated and strives to do well in school.
22. **Learning engagement**—Child is responsive, attentive, and actively engaged in learning at school and enjoys participating in learning activities outside of school.
23. **Homework**—Child usually hands in homework on time.
24. **Bonding to adults at school**—Child cares about teachers and other adults at school.
25. **Reading for pleasure**—Child enjoys and engages in reading for fun most days of the week.

POSITIVE VALUES

26. **Caring**—Parent(s) tell the child it is important to help other people.
27. **Equality and social justice**—Parent(s) tell the child it is important to speak up for equal rights for all people.
28. **Integrity**—Parent(s) tell the child it is important to stand up for one's beliefs.
29. **Honesty**—Parent(s) tell the child it is important to tell the truth.
30. **Responsibility**—Parent(s) tell the child it is important to accept personal responsibility for behavior.
31. **Healthy lifestyle**—Parent(s) tell the child it is important to have good health habits and an understanding of healthy sexuality.

SOCIAL COMPETENCIES

32. **Planning and decision making**—Child thinks about decisions and is usually happy with results of her or his decisions.
33. **Interpersonal competence**—Child cares about and is affected by other people's feelings, enjoys making friends, and, when frustrated or angry, tries to calm her- or himself.
34. **Cultural competence**—Child knows and is comfortable with people of different racial, ethnic, and cultural backgrounds and with her or his own cultural identity.
35. **Resistance skills**—Child can stay away from people who are likely to get her or him in trouble and is able to say no to doing wrong or dangerous things.
36. **Peaceful conflict resolution**—Child attempts to resolve conflict nonviolently.

POSITIVE IDENTITY

37. **Personal power**—Child feels he or she has some influence over things that happen in her or his life.
38. **Self-esteem**—Child likes and is proud to be the person he or she is.
39. **Sense of purpose**—Child sometimes thinks about what life means and whether there is a purpose for her or his life.
40. **Positive view of personal future**—Child is optimistic about her or his personal future.

PART 1

Using the Developmental Assets Framework to Build Community with Kids

Chapter 1

Building an Understanding of the Developmental Assets Framework

The activities in this chapter help young people make

connections that build an early understanding of the

developmental assets and why they are important.

This chapter sets the stage and invites participants

to engage with the material by having them

ask questions and make predictions.

1 — A PACK FULL OF ASSETS

Focus

By making connections with their own experiences, young people develop an understanding of the developmental assets for middle childhood and know why they are important.

Materials

- [ ] One student backpack filled with school supplies, such as textbooks, notebooks, binders, folders, homework assignments, pencils, pens, erasers, rulers, and colored markers
- [ ] Pens or pencils
- [ ] "A Pack Full of Assets" Activity Sheet

Activity

Hold up the backpack and invite children to predict what items might be inside. Ask: *What do students need so they can do their very best in school?* Use additional questions that encourage the children to share the reasons behind their predictions:

- Why do you think we'll find a (book, pencil, notebook, homework assignment, etc.) in the backpack?
- Why does a student need this item?
- How do these things help a student succeed in school?

Once the children have named and discussed a majority of items in the backpack, open up the backpack to show all the different school supplies. Acknowledge that kids need a lot of different materials to do well in school. Be sure to make note of useful items the children suggested that aren't contained in the backpack. Also reveal the items in the backpack that the children did not predict and encourage participants to describe how each item can help a student do her or his best at school.

Next, challenge the children to think beyond objects that fit in a backpack: *Besides school supplies, what else do kids need to bring to school to be successful learners?* Help them create a list that includes such ideas as positive attitude, desire to learn, attentive listening, willingness to work hard, and cooperation. Expand the backpack example beyond school by asking: *What do young people need to do their very best in life?*

Introduce children to the word *assets* by explaining that the term is one way we can describe items of value that belong to us. Sometimes things are valuable to us because we paid money for them, like the school supplies in the backpack, or our clothes, or a car, or a house. But the word *assets* also describes things we don't pay money for but that make our lives rich in other ways. "Friends we can trust" is one example of a valuable asset.

Invite young people to brainstorm a list of other examples, reminding participants that the goal of brainstorming is to collect lots of ideas, rather than to decide on right or wrong responses. Ideas on the list could include a loving family, helpful neighbors, enjoyment of reading, and the desire to help others.

Return to the backpack analogy. Encourage the young people to connect the idea of the backpack with the concept of assets by suggesting: *You can think of yourself as a backpack that you want to fill with assets. These assets are things that are valuable to you and will help you do your very best in life.*

Distribute the "A Pack Full of Assets" Activity Sheet. Ask each young person to think about the assets in her or his own life. Have them record their responses inside the "life pack." After several minutes, ask for volunteers to share some of the concrete, personal examples recorded on the activity sheet.

A Pack Full of Assets

What do you need to do your very best in life? Use words and pictures to fill your "life pack" with those things that will help you become a caring and thoughtful person.

2 — COOKING UP MY ASSETS

Focus
Participants develop a deeper understanding of the asset framework by learning the difference between internal and external assets.

Materials
- ☐ Large soup kettle or pot
- ☐ Each asset category name printed in bold letters on an index card: Support, Empowerment, Boundaries and Expectations, Constructive Use of Time, Commitment to Learning, Positive Values, Social Competencies, and Positive Identity
- ☐ Pens or pencils
- ☐ "Cooking Up My Assets" Activity Sheet

Activity
Place soup kettle in front of the group, and ask children to brainstorm a list of items they might need to make a pot of soup. Be sure that they mention not only the ingredients that go into the pot (chicken, noodles, spices, etc.) but also the necessary equipment to make the soup (knife, cutting board, spoon, stove, power for stove, etc.). Talk about the difference between the ingredients that go inside the pot and the utensils that make cooking possible. Explain that a person needs both *internal* ingredients and *external* utensils and tools to make a good soup.

Hold up each of the eight asset category cards one at a time and read the brief descriptions that appear below. (Use the list on page 9 if you would like to share the complete definitions of all 40 assets.)

As you define each category (see below), emphasize why it is an external (happens around you) or internal (happens inside you) category. Explain that like a good soup, a healthy young person also requires external help as well as high-quality internal ingredients.

To further reinforce an understanding of the concept of internal and external assets, let the children pretend to make soup using the cards. Invite volunteers to verbally review the eight asset categories. After a volunteer describes an asset category, ask her or him to determine whether the category is internal or external. Volunteers should then place internal assets inside the kettle and external assets just outside the kettle. After all eight asset categories are placed correctly, invite a final volunteer to "stir" the soup by using one of the external asset cards as a pretend spoon. Pretend to smell something really good: *I smell the makings of a really cool kid in this "soup"!*

Use the "Cooking Up My Assets" Activity Sheet to help young people identify examples of external and internal assets in their own lives. Invite the children to share their "soup" with the group. Give them an opportunity to add more "ingredients" after all have had a chance to share. Display their "kettles."

Optional Variation
If your group of young people meets in a space that has a stove, hot plate, or electric cooking pot, consider actually making a simple soup while doing this activity.

THE DEVELOPMENTAL ASSETS

External Assets
- **Support**
  You have a family, a neighborhood, and a school made up of people who care about you.
- **Empowerment**
  You feel like a valuable person in your community, and you feel safe in your home, neighborhood, and school.
- **Boundaries and Expectations**
  The adults and other children in your life expect you to do your best and follow certain rules.
- **Constructive Use of Time**
  You are involved in creative activities or programs inside and outside your home.

Internal Assets
- **Commitment to Learning**
  You care about homework, enjoy reading for fun, and like learning new things.
- **Positive Values**
  Your parents or guardians have taught you to be honest and responsible. You know it is important to treat people equally and respectfully.
- **Social Competencies**
  You know how to make good decisions and get along with people. When you have problems, you try to solve them without using violence.
- **Positive Identity**
  You feel good about yourself and believe that you can do some things very well.

Cooking Up My Assets

Consider the different kinds of assets that children need as they grow up. *External* assets are positive experiences and qualities that come from outside you, such as having a family that cares about you, feeling safe in your neighborhood, having positive role models, and being involved in creative activities or programs. *Internal* assets are qualities you experience within you, such as a desire to learn, caring about other people, being a good friend, and feeling proud of yourself.

Think about what helps you be the best person you can be. On the outside of the kettle, write or draw the external assets you experience from outside yourself. Inside the kettle, write or draw the internal assets that help you on the inside.

Chapter 2

Building Community within Your Group

Use the activities in this chapter to build a caring community among group members. Once young people establish familiarity, trust, and respect among themselves, they will work together to support and encourage each other's efforts to build assets for themselves and with others.

Focus

Participants build positive relationships with peers.

Activity

Share with your group the following quote by professional golfer Tiger Woods on how he built a caring relationship with his father:

> *We would sit there and talk for hours. That's how we built up trust and respect for each other.*

Explain that Tiger Woods tells us that talking can actually be a lot more important than it might seem. You don't always have to be doing something with somebody other than just talking to truly get to know and trust that person.

Suggest to your group that when young people share stories from their lives, they learn how to listen to what is meaningful in another person's life. They get to know each other and identify connections that build caring relationships. A Go-Around story session provides a structure that gives each child a chance to listen and a chance to share.

Direct the young people to sit in small-group circles. Invite them to share stories that will help them get to know each other. Introduce a story topic from the list provided, or invite the children to suggest a topic. To start sharing stories, you may also read a story (see sample) or tell a story from your own life. Ask group members to go around the circle as each person takes a turn telling her or his story while the others listen.

Emphasize that while the story can be funny or embarrassing, it doesn't need to be. Encourage the children to share stories that are meaningful to them. Remind the group that this activity is a way to get to know each other and build trust. Invite the storyteller to comment on any lessons learned or relationships that changed during the experience described in the story.

Model and affirm positive communication skills during your story sessions. Tell children that this is an opportunity to practice listening and asking questions, not a time to judge and criticize. Assure students that it's okay to pass if they feel uncomfortable. Be sure to redirect any unkind comments. Thank the children for sharing their stories and for listening kindly to each other's important stories.

Go-Around Story Topics

- Animal Antics (Pet Stories)
- Birthday Surprise or Wish
- Kitchen Disasters or Cooking Mishaps
- My Ideal Day
- When I Was a Baby . . .
- Things That Give Me Goose Bumps (Terror Tales)
- A Time When You Had a Lot of Fun When You Didn't Expect To
- Travel Adventures
- Worst Wound

Sample Go-Around Stories to Start Story Sessions

Birthday Surprise (shared by an adult)

> *When I was in elementary school, my friend's mom planned a treasure hunt for my friend's birthday party. We had to follow clues all around the park and try to discover the treasure. It started pouring rain during the hunt, but the mud made the adventure even more fun! My team solved the clues and found the treasure before anyone else did. We won some cool necklaces and candy.*

Kitchen Disaster (shared by a 5th grader)

> *When I was about three years old, I wanted a treat but my mom said no. She said what all moms say, "It will spoil your dinner." I was mad. When she left the kitchen to check on the laundry, I snuck into the refrigerator and grabbed the first thing on the shelf. I took a huge bite before she could come back and catch me. It turned out to be an onion. I was gagging and crying when my mom came back in the room.*

Worst Wound (shared by a 4th grader)

> *When I was about four years old, I wanted to fly like Peter Pan. I climbed up on the back of the couch and jumped as high as I could. But I found out I couldn't fly after all. I fell on the corner of a low table and had to go to the doctor to get four stitches.*

Optional Variation

Invite other staff or multigenerational groups to join in.

Focus

Children learn that building positive relationships requires showing support in word and deed.

Materials

For each small group of four children, you will need:

- [ ] An equal number of building blocks: Legos, K'Nex, or Lincoln Logs
- [ ] Several hardcover books of the same approximate weight
- [ ] Note cards

Advance Preparations

Create a collection of note cards marked with directions for role playing. Each card should list one direction for being either a helpful group member or a disruptive one. Use the following examples or make up your own:

- Praise people in your group for their good ideas.
- Ask someone in your group who has been quiet to share her or his ideas.
- Suggest that each person take a turn sharing her or his ideas.
- Encourage your group to work as a team.
- Play with the blocks to try to make someone laugh.
- Leave your group and wander around the room to avoid helping.
- Try to convince everyone to agree with your ideas. Take over. Act bossy.
- Talk about other topics to try to distract one person in your group.

Activity

Divide children into small groups of four. Invite them to use building blocks to create a strong structure that will support the weight of several books. Let group members get started on their construction projects.

Next, give one or two members of each team a note card with a role-playing suggestion. Ask each person who receives a card to read the information without revealing its contents to anyone else; instruct them to start using the behavior or attitude described on the card.

After several minutes, ask the groups to stop. Invite them to reflect on their group experience, using such questions as:

- What thoughts and feelings did you experience while working on your construction project?
- What led you to feel frustrated? What prevented your group from working well together?
- What supportive actions and messages did you observe during your group's work time?

Collect the role cards and redistribute them to different children in each group. Direct participants to resume building their structures, letting them know how much time they have left to complete the structure. Halt construction and see how many books each structure can hold. Encourage participants to continue using their role cards during the weight test.

Repeat the questions above, and add the following:

- Was your group able to complete the task in the time allowed?
- Did the role cards affect how successful your project was? Why or why not?
- Which role cards made construction harder and why?
- Which role cards made construction easier and why?
- What ideas do you have for helping groups work well together?

PART 2

External Assets

Chapter 3

Support

Everyone needs to feel loved, appreciated, accepted,
and included. Use this chapter to help young people
recognize different forms of support and to
identify the people who support them.

Family Support (Asset 1)

Focus
Children define and describe family support. They identify how words and actions demonstrate love and support.

Materials
- [ ] Nonfiction books that include descriptions of animal families. Possible examples include:
  - ➤ *The Octopus: Phantom of the Sea* by Mary Cerullo (Penguin Putnam Books, 1997)
  - ➤ *Animal Babies* by John Wexo (Zoobooks/Wildlife Education, 2001)
- [ ] "Octopus of Support" Activity Sheet

Advance Preparations
Select nonfiction books about animals and mark the sections that describe animal families. (If you are working with older children, you may prefer to let them use the index to locate these sections on their own, but you should still confirm that the books contain this information.)

Activity
Have young people break up into small groups and read aloud from nonfiction books about ways different types of animals care for their young. Then gather the children back together to explore the concept of family support. Ask:
- How do animal babies rely on their parents?
- How do various types of animals care for their young?
- How do animal siblings play together? What about animal aunts and uncles?
- What are some similarities between the ways animals care for their young and humans care for their young?
- How do the people in your family provide care and support for you?

Ask young people to imagine that a family is like an octopus with lots of arms that offer different kinds of support. Encourage the children to think about the different forms of family support by asking:
- What do parents and guardians *do* to show their children love and support? (actions)
- What do parents and guardians *say* to show their children love and support? (messages)

Note that both actions and messages are necessary for families to work well together. Distribute the "Octopus of Support" Activity Sheet for the children to take home. Invite the kids to talk with family members to collect actions and messages that reveal how their own families show love and support. Encourage them to write one specific example on each arm of the octopus. Ask the children to bring back their "Octopus of Support" Activity Sheet when your group meets again. Use the sheets as a springboard for the young people to share what they learned about family support.

Octopus of Support

Families support children using both words and actions. Imagine that a family is like an octopus, and each arm is one way that a family gives support. On each arm of the octopus below, write one example of how someone in your family gives you love and support. Include encouraging statements family members *say* to you as well as supportive actions that your family members *do*.

Family Support (Asset 1)

Focus

Children recognize support as a basic human need, list other basic human needs, and distinguish between needs and wants.

Materials

☐ Bag of props with items that represent needs (a toothbrush, an apple, mittens, etc.) and wants (a toy, candy, a compact disc, etc.)

☐ Notebooks or journals

☐ Pens or pencils

☐ "What a Kid Needs, What a Kid Wants" Activity Sheet

Activity

Invite different children to take a prop out of the prop bag and decide whether it belongs in a pile of needs or wants. Ask the children to define *needs* and *wants:* A *need* is something that is necessary for a healthy life, such as food, clothing, shelter, and love; a *want* is something that would enrich your life. Encourage the participants to list synonyms for each word. For example, a *need* is also a requirement or a must; a *want* is also a desire or a wish.

Ask participants to describe situations associated with needs and wants. Stress that needs include physical as well as emotional necessities, such as love and encouragement.

Ask the young people to write the following sentence starter in their journal: "I need . . ." Give them about five minutes to brainstorm a list of ideas. Then ask them to write another sentence starter on the page: "I want . . ." Give them another five minutes to brainstorm ideas. Invite the children to share their lists.

Explore needs and wants by asking:
• How do you think your list of needs and wants might change as you grow older?
• What needs would be on a newborn's list? a toddler's list? a teen's list? an adult's list?
• What needs and wants would your parents, guardians, or caregivers identify for you? How do they differ from what you want?
• What are examples of needs that you will require throughout your life?

Distribute the "What a Kid Needs, What a Kid Wants" Activity Sheet to each participant. Explain that while there are some needs and wants we can provide for ourselves, everyone needs help from others in getting all their needs and wants met.

What a Kid Needs,
What a Kid Wants

Think about what you *need* to do well in life and what you *want*. Use the diagram below to sort your needs from your wants.

- **Which needs can you take care of on your own?**
  List these needs in the circle on the left.

- **Which needs require help from your family?**
  List these needs in the circle on the right.

- **Which needs might fall somewhere in the middle?**
  List these needs in the space where the two circles overlap.

- **What about the things you want?**
  List these things outside of the circles.

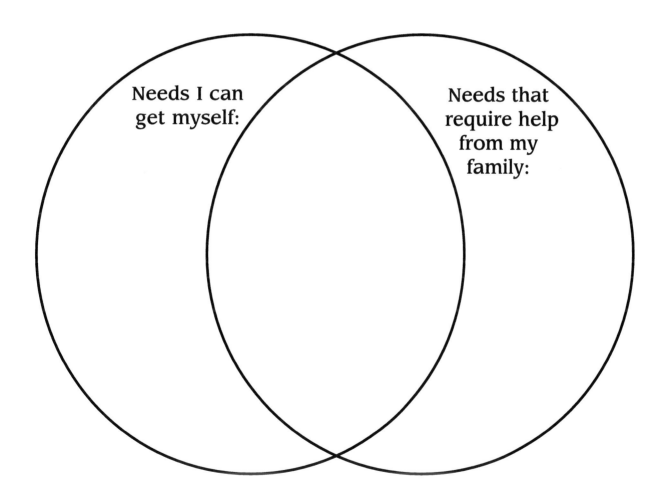

Needs I can get myself:

Needs that require help from my family:

Positive Family Communication (Asset 2)

Focus
Children role-play building positive communication skills and supportive interactions with family members.

Materials
- ☐ Radio
- ☐ Pencils or pens
- ☐ One set of headphones (to be used as a prop)
- ☐ One telephone receiver (to be used as a prop)
- ☐ "Talk Radio" Activity Sheet

Activity
Turn on the radio. Ask kids to name a favorite station and adjust the tuning dial to that station. Then adjust the dial to get static. Repeat this procedure a couple of times. Explain:

Sometimes you can tune in a strong radio signal and hear the music or talking clearly. Other times the message is fuzzy and hard to hear. Communication in families works the same way: Sometimes we understand each other clearly, and other times what we are trying to say to one another is hard to understand because we have trouble saying what we mean or listening to each other.

Invite young people to work in small groups to address the following questions:
- What skills do you need to communicate with others?
- Why is it sometimes difficult to communicate within families?
- How can you open the lines of communication?
- How can you tune in to your parents' or guardians' "radio station"—to what they are thinking, feeling, and saying?

- How can you help them tune in to your "station"—what you're thinking, feeling, saying?

Distribute the "Talk Radio" Activity Sheet. Ask the children to imagine creating a radio show for their families to hear. Ask them to use the first script card to list song titles that they'd like to play for their families along with possible DJ comments. Encourage the participants to think of real song titles or make up imaginary ones that express their wants, needs, hopes, and emotions. Share some sample titles to help them get started. To communicate with a parent or guardian, a young person might, for example, use some of the following titles: "I Know I Can," "Complicated," or "Where Is the Love?"

Then ask participants to pretend to be one of their own family members (parent, guardian, or sibling). Invite participants to use the second script card to generate family members' call-in comments and requested songs. Examples of parental requests might include "You Are My Sunshine," "Sure Could Use a Little Good News Today," or "Messy Bedroom Blues"; sibling requests might include "My Sister Is Great," "You Really Bug Me," or "My Little Brother Looks Up to Me."

Ask for volunteers to come to the front of the room to act out the radio show. Direct the young people to wear the headphones while announcing songs and delivering the DJ lines or to use the telephone to role-play a family member calling in to ask questions and request songs. Explain that the script card is just a way to help the kids get started; encourage them to add new titles or questions as they role-play. Allow as many participants as possible to have a turn.

Talk Radio

Young Person/DJ's Script Card

DJ: Welcome to WFAM, where we play songs to meet the needs of the family. I'm your host, _____. First I'd like to play a couple of songs about my needs. The song titles are _____ and _____. I am playing these songs because _____ _____

Now that I have let you know my needs, I am accepting requests from my listeners. Oh! I think I have a call on line one. What's on your mind, caller?

Family Member/Radio Listener's Script Card

Family Member: Thanks, DJ. I was listening just now when you played the song _____, and it made me feel _____. I am glad that you played the song so I know how you feel, but I have a question about it: _____ _____? Also, I would like to request a song of my own: _____. I am requesting it because _____ _____.

Thanks for including me on your show!

EXTERNAL ASSETS: SUPPORT

Positive Family Communication (Asset 2)

Focus

Participants learn to concentrate on listening during family discussions.

Materials

☐ Large brown paper bags

☐ Scissors

☐ Crayons or markers

Activity

Invite young people to use the paper bags to make masks, but explain that they should cut only two holes in the mask: ear holes. They should *not* cut holes for the eyes, nose, or mouth. Let them decorate the mask with a face and hair.

Once the children have decorated their masks, ask for two volunteers to role-play a scenario of family communication. Ask someone else in the group to suggest an emotion or a situation that a family member may wish to discuss, and assign roles to the volunteers. One example: a discussion between a family member who wants to keep the family cat's new litter of kittens and another family member who wants to give them away.

Let one volunteer act the part of a family member who needs to talk and share feelings, while the other volunteer wears her or his mask and listens quietly. Explain that because the mask has no mouth, the volunteer must remain silent during the exercise, but needs to listen carefully.

When the speaker finishes, the volunteers should change roles. The former listener takes off the mask and speaks, while the former speaker dons the mask and listens.

Ask the volunteers:

- How did it feel to simply listen and not make comments while the other person spoke?
- How did it feel to speak, knowing you would not be interrupted?

Ask the children who were watching the role play:

- Do you think both of these people had a chance to say how they felt? Why or why not?

Ask everyone:

- How are you a good listener?
- What are some things you might do that makes it hard for someone else to express her or his feelings?
- How do the people in your family communicate? How well do they listen? Does each member of your family get a chance to say how he or she feels?

Let everyone pair off and take turns role-playing. Suggest some of the following topics or encourage the kids to brainstorm their own ideas.

- A child requests a later bedtime; the parent or guardian says the child is not getting enough sleep.
- An older sibling has moved out of the house, leaving the best bedroom free. Two siblings argue, each contending he or she is the most deserving of the room.
- A parent explains that the family rule is "homework must be done before going outside to play"; the child argues for an exception, "just for tonight."

Gather the participants together and ask them to share insights from their role play. Ask them to name things people do to make it easy to listen or hard to listen. Invite them to share what they will do in the future to be a better listener.

⑨ SHELTERING TREE STATIONERY

Other Adult Relationships (Asset 3)

Focus
Children identify the value of and show appreciation for supportive relationships with adults other than their parents.

Materials
- ☐ Sample thank-you cards
- ☐ Paper and envelopes
- ☐ Crayons, markers, or colored pencils
- ☐ Other fun art materials, such as stickers, ink stamps, craft scissors that cut designs, shaped hole punches, glitter, and colored glue

Advance Preparations
Making comparisons helps young people turn abstract concepts into something visual and concrete. To help your young participants explore similes and metaphors for love and support, create a greeting card or stationery letterhead using sheltering trees as a metaphor for supportive friendship. You may prefer to choose some other metaphor than sheltering trees to illustrate love and support. Identify an adult other than a parent who shows you love and support through words and deeds. Use your greeting card or stationery to write this valued adult a thank-you card.

Activity
Show the young people in your group the thank-you card you have made and read the message aloud. Describe the intended recipient of the card, and ask the group to think about why you designed your card the way you did. If the participants do not find meaning in the image of a sheltering tree, you may need to explain how a tree's branches can be strong, supportive, or protective. No matter what simile or metaphor you choose, be sure that you help your group make these connections. Explain that using metaphors and similes means comparing two things to show that they are alike.

Share additional samples of thank-you cards from stationery stores. Encourage young people to read the cards and look over the illustrations and words inside. Use these questions to guide your discussion:
- What kinds of cards do you like to receive?
- What kinds of cards do you like to give?
- What kinds of thank-you cards or letters have you received?
- What kinds of messages in the letters touched your heart?

Invite the children to identify the supportive adults in their lives by asking:
- Who deserves to be appreciated for giving you love and support?
- How can you thank this person?
- For what specific words and deeds would you like to thank this person?

Encourage participants to make comparisons that describe their thoughts and feelings about supportive relationships in their lives. Invite them to use the following sentence starters to brainstorm similes:
- Family is like . . .
- Friends are like . . .
- Love is like . . .
- Support is like . . .

Ask participants to share their simile sentences. Invite them to imagine how they can use the brainstormed ideas to create thank-you cards for adults who have shown them love and support. They might transform the same similes into more personal statements using the following sentence starters:
- Your love is like . . .
- Your support is like . . .
- Our relationship is like . . .

Have participants create thank-you cards and write messages to adults who have shown them love and support. Suggest that they draw pictures based on their simile sentences and include the simile sentences as text on their letter or card. Encourage them to deliver at least one card to a supportive adult who is not a parent or guardian.

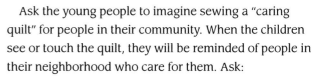

Caring Neighborhood (Asset 4)

Focus
Children identify ways to show their support for others in a neighborhood.

Materials
- ☐ 12-inch squares of light-colored fabric
- ☐ Needles, thread, thimbles
- ☐ Sample quilt or quilt square that depicts an image
- ☐ Patches of colored fabric, fabric paint, fabric pens or permanent acrylic markers, and fabric glue for decorating quilt squares
- ☐ One or more children's fiction books about quilts. Suggestions of books in which quilting is the source of a supportive relationship between two or more people include:
  - ➤ *The Patchwork Quilt* by Valerie Flournoy (Penguin Putnam, 1985)
  - ➤ *The Keeping Quilt* by Patricia Polacco (Simon & Schuster, 1998)
  - ➤ *Sweet Clara and the Freedom Quilt* by Deborah Hopkinson (Knopf, 1995)
- ☐ Yarn, sequins, or other decorative objects (optional)
- ☐ Experienced quilter to assist the group (optional)

Activity
Read aloud the book that you have chosen, and encourage young people to share responses to the story. Pass around the sample quilt or quilt square. Ask:
- How is love like a quilt?
- How is support like a quilt?
- How is a neighborhood like a quilt?

Explain that a neighborhood is like a quilt that is made by many different people: Each person contributes her or his gifts to create a positive, healthy place for everyone to live.

Ask the young people to imagine sewing a "caring quilt" for people in their community. When the children see or touch the quilt, they will be reminded of people in their neighborhood who care for them. Ask:
- What pictures would you draw on a quilt square to show the positive contributions you make to your neighborhood?
- What words or phrases would you add to your square?
- How will the quilt show that someone can count on you for support?

Invite each child to create a single quilt square that shows how he or she expresses love and support in the neighborhood. Depending on the skill levels of your participants and the resources available, you may find that it is easier for a young person to draw on a quilt square or glue items on the square instead of sewing smaller pieces together. Arrange the finished squares into a grid. Let the young people take turns using needle and thread to bind the squares together to create a quilt of caring. If necessary, an experienced quilter can provide sewing tips.

Investigate the possibility of displaying the quilt somewhere in the neighborhood, such as at a library, community center, or even a shopping mall.

Optional Variation
Make quilt squares out of construction paper or felt. Draw designs with markers or glue pieces of colored paper or felt shapes to the quilt squares. Supplies could include three-dimensional objects such as feathers, beads, or glitter. Use double-sided masking tape to mount the squares to the wall in a grid pattern.

⑪— FRIENDSHIP SANDWICH

Caring School Climate (Asset 5)

Focus
Participants work to make their school climate welcoming and caring.

Materials
☐ Note cards
☐ "Friendship Sandwich" Activity Sheet

Advance Preparations
Create sets of six note cards (enough for every group member to receive one card). On each note card, write one of the following questions:
- Do you ever feel as if you are alone at lunchtime even when you're sitting with others?
- How does it feel to eat lunch without any of your friends nearby?
- If you see someone eating alone, do you ever want to invite that person to eat with you? Why or why not? What kinds of things could you say if you wanted to invite someone to sit with you at lunch?
- What is it like to invite *yourself* to sit with other people? What makes that hard to do? What makes that easy to do?
- What kinds of things could you say if you wanted to sit with some kids you don't usually sit with?
- What are some good things you might experience from meeting new people? How might a person benefit from your invitation to sit with you?

Place each set of cards in a cluster or a circle where young people can sit, marking each seat with one card. You may need to move chairs or desks to accommodate this arrangement.

Activity
As children arrive, invite them to pick a seat. Ask them to notice whether the children they have chosen to sit with are children they know well.

Instruct the participants to start small-group discussions in which each person has an opportunity to ask the question on her or his note card. Invite each group to report back to the large group about what they learned from their discussion about making new friends.

Next, invite the children to stand up and move to a different spot and sit with a different group of children. Again, ask them to note to themselves whether the children they have chosen to sit with are children they know well.

Distribute the "Friendship Sandwich" Activity Sheet to help students think about the friendship choices they make during lunchtime. As they fill in the names of people who usually sit with them and the names of people whom they will invite to join them, suggest that they include people they do not know very well. Encourage the young people to make a promise to themselves that they will be more inviting and welcoming during lunchtime and whenever they are selecting groups.

Friendship Sandwich

Write your name in the middle of the sandwich. On the bottom piece of bread, write the names of the people who usually sit with you during lunch. On the top piece of bread, write the name of at least two additional people whom you will invite to sit with you.

⑫ SUNNY SCHOOL

Caring School Climate (Asset 5)

Focus
Children interview people in their schools to identify factors that contribute to a climate of caring and encouragement.

Materials
- ☐ Pens or pencils
- ☐ Newsprint paper
- ☐ Masking tape

For each small group of four to six students:
- ☐ Information about local weather: weather maps, weather forecast in the daily newspaper, chart with average temperature highs and lows printed from the Internet, etc.
- ☐ "Sunny School" Activity Sheet

Activity
Divide children into small groups and ask them to study the local weather materials. Ask each group to determine what the weather prediction is for today and to identify what factors, such as winds, season, and latitude, go into making a weather prediction. Ask: *For a meteorologist to predict a sunny day, what factors need to be present (or absent)?* Review the idea that although weather is not completely predictable, meteorologists can use several factors to help them determine what the weather will be like.

Then ask: *For the mood of a classroom to be "sunny" or caring, what conditions need to be present?* Suggest that sometimes the mood inside a room or a building can be similar to the way weather patterns feel to you outside. Negative attitudes can be like dangerous winds or loud thunder, and friendly actions can be like pleasant sunshine. Explain that the word for this similarity is *climate*. Whether you are predicting the weather outside or the way people might feel in a particular room or building or setting, you can look around at different factors to predict the climate.

Ask each group to look around the room and identify what factors help predict a "sunny" climate for your meeting. Gather the children back together for a large-group discussion. Invite a "meteorologist" from several of the small groups to share what conditions help predict a caring climate inside the room.

Hand out the "Sunny School" Activity Sheet. Help the young people brainstorm factors that would help contribute to and encourage a sunny feeling in school; these should be positive statements with which someone could agree or disagree. Encourage the children to generate as many statements as possible. Starter suggestions include:
- Our school is clean.
- Our school feels friendly.
- I feel safe when I am at school.
- Our school is accepting of many different kinds of kids.

When the children all agree to a statement, have them write it in the left column of the "Sunny School" Activity Sheet.

Instruct the children to take the partially completed activity sheet and interview five people: at least one child of a different age, at least one teacher, and at least one other adult staff person. (If the children are not presently at their school, ask them to complete the survey at school and bring it back to a later meeting.) Have the children record tally marks on the chart to see how many people agree with each statement. Once the young people return, discuss and compare everyone's results to gain a broader understanding of school climate. Tape newsprint paper to the front of the room to record all the results on a master chart and look for patterns.

Introduce the idea that because predictable factors go into making sunny weather, the children can take steps to influence the climate or feeling inside their school. Ask the kids to address the question: *What can I do to help create a sunny school?* Brainstorm ideas that the children can do themselves to improve climate, using the survey results as a starting point. Encourage the young people to share the survey results with the school principal or other administrator, along with their suggestions for making the "local weather" even better.

Sunny School

In the left column below, list several positive statements that could help encourage "sunny weather" and a caring climate in your school. Read these statements to five other people in your school—both youth and adults. Ask them to rate their feelings about each statement and record the answers in the appropriate boxes using tally marks.

"Sunny Weather" Predictors	Strongly Disagree	Disagree	Agree	Strongly Agree
Adults in our school are respectful toward young people.				

Parent Involvement in Schooling (Asset 6)

Focus
Participants ask parents or guardians to share information about their school days.

Materials
☐ Pens or pencils
☐ "When I Was Your Age . . ." Activity Sheet

Activity
Begin with a large-group discussion about the ways that schools have changed between generations. Use the following questions to start your discussion:

- How do you think school was different for your parents or guardians than it is for you? How do you think it was the same?
- What do you know about the time that your parents or guardians spent at school?
- What information would you like to know?

Pass out the "When I Was Your Age . . ." Activity Sheet. In addition to the questions listed on the activity sheet, ask children to brainstorm other possible questions to ask. Invite them to add two of the brainstormed questions to the bottom of their activity sheets.

Instruct the children to use the activity sheet to interview their parents or guardians, and then bring the completed sheets back to the group. Invite volunteers to share what they learned about how school used to be. Ask:

- Do you think the way school has changed is an improvement or not? Why or why not?
- Are there any lessons from your parents' or guardians' school days that might be useful for schools to adopt today?

"When I Was Your Age . . ."

Use the questions below to interview your parent or guardian. Add your own questions on the bottom lines.

1. What was your school's name?

2. What were your favorite classes or subject areas?

3. How much homework did you get?

4. Did your parents or guardians help you with your homework?

5. Which teacher had a positive impact on you? Why?

6. What was the most challenging part of school for you?

7. What differences do you see between your school and my school?

8. _____

9. _____

14 — FAMILY HISTORY LIVE!

Parent Involvement in Schooling (Asset 6)

Focus
Young people invite parents or guardians to participate in an activity at school.

Materials
- ☐ Paper
- ☐ Pens or pencils
- ☐ One audiocassette for every participating young person
- ☐ Several audiocassette recorders
- ☐ "Family History Live!" Activity Sheet

Advance Preparations
Asset 6 describes the importance of parent involvement *at school;* if you work in a youth-serving program outside of a school, you may want to try to coordinate with a teacher or school administrator to schedule this event at the school that most or many of your participants attend.

Note that children will need to create and deliver their invitations (the activity sheet) to parents or guardians in advance. To plan for numbers attending the event, or if your organization requires permission slips, you might consider including it in the form of an RSVP with the invitation.

On the day of the recording session, make sure that all of the audiocassette recorders function properly.

Activity
Inform the children that they will be helping to plan a family history event at school. Use the following questions to generate a discussion about family history:
- Who are the people in your family?
- What different ways have people become new members of your family? Marriage? Birth? Adoption? Close friendships (de facto members)?
- What do you know about the history of your family?
- In which countries did your ancestors live?

- Are there any names in your family that have special meanings?
- What is something you wish you knew about your parents' or guardians' childhood experiences?

Pass out paper and pencils and instruct the participants to brainstorm a list of family history questions to ask their parents or guardians. Encourage them to consider topics from the initial discussion, and mention additional subjects, such as ethnic history, extended families, immigration, religion, or neighborhoods. Have each student list several questions to ask her or his parent(s) or guardian(s).

Distribute the "Family History Live!" Activity Sheet. Let children fill in the blanks (the agreed-upon time and location and interview questions). Then ask them to bring this sheet home as an invitation to their parents and guardians. If a parent or guardian is not available to attend, children may invite an older sibling, extended family member, or family friend. Children may need to adjust their lists of questions based on whom they will be inviting.

When parents and guardians arrive at the family history event, ask the child/parent teams to form small groups with other child/parent teams. Give each small group an audiocassette recorder. Explain that each child will take a turn with the audiocassette recorder, placing her or his own tape in the recorder, asking the interview questions, and tape-recording the responses. Other child/parent teams are invited to listen and wait their turn. Encourage parents and guardians to participate actively and to elaborate on their answers or offer additional information as time allows.

Instruct each child to label the tape with her or his name, the name of the person interviewed, and the date. Let each family keep the family history tape for posterity. Encourage families to record more interviews on the tape with other family members at a later time.

Family History Live!

You are invited to a special

Family History Live!

recording session.

Location: _____

Date: _____

Time: _____

We will be recording an audiotape about our family history. I would like to interview you to learn facts and stories about our family. Below are some of the questions I will be asking you during the interview:

1. _____

2. _____

3. _____

4. _____

5. _____

EXTERNAL ASSETS: SUPPORT

Chapter 4

Empowerment

Young people need to feel that they can contribute

to their world in a positive way. The activities

in this chapter provide opportunities for

participants to exercise power and

responsibility in safe, meaningful ways.

Community Values Children (Asset 7)

Focus
Children envision a neighborhood that values them.

Materials
☐ One large box for every two to four young people (obtain a set of cardboard boxes of about equal size at the grocery or hardware store)
☐ Assorted art supplies, such as paints, markers, paper, scissors, and glue
☐ "Found" items, such as paper towel tubes, smaller boxes, and bottle caps

Activity
Arrange the boxes as if they are buildings lining the intersection of a street. Invite the children to arrange their chairs in a circle surrounding the boxes. Ask the children:
- What are some of the different buildings you see in your neighborhood? What kinds of businesses or organizations do they represent?
- Who are some of the people you know who work in these buildings?
- Which businesses and organizations in your community do you feel value kids? How do they make you feel valued?
- How could citizens in a community show that they value young people?

Invite the children to design a neighborhood in which children feel valued. Divide them into small groups or pairs, and give each group one box. Ask each team to construct one example of a place that would exist in a community that values its young people, using art supplies and "found" items. Encourage them to think beyond schools and youth-serving organizations. Possibilities might include a post office that issues stamps designed by children, a bank that offers special checking accounts for young people, or a bookstore or library that has a special section for children and invites children's authors to give readings.

Once the groups have constructed their buildings, re-assemble them in two rows to represent the Main Street of their imaginary community. Ask the participants to describe their buildings to the larger group and to explain how each place contributes to a caring community.

Optional Variation
If you can obtain refrigerator-size boxes from an appliance store, have the children actually run the various businesses and organizations from inside their box creations. For example, have the bank issue pretend money. Children can use the money to buy child-designed stamps at the post office to send child-designed cards to other community members. Discuss how it feels to live in a community that values young people.

16 — I CARE CARDS

Children as Resources (Asset 8)

Focus

Children communicate with people in their communities and identify useful roles for themselves at home and in the neighborhood.

Materials

☐ Paper or cardstock (unlined index cards)
☐ Pens or pencils
☐ Sample business cards

Advance Preparations

Collect sample business cards. Try to include cards from people who provide a wide variety of services. You may also wish to invite your group members to bring the business cards of their parents, guardians, or other caring adults in their lives.

Activity

Share sample business cards with the young people in your group. Circulate the cards, and ask your group members to identify the kinds of information that business cards include. Talk about how adults use business cards to network and to use other people as resources. Ask the group to brainstorm a list of services that they might be able to offer on a business card. Use the following questions to help them generate ideas:

- What are some things that you are good at doing?
- What are some chores that you know how to do?
- How could you use your talents and abilities to help other people?

Invite participants to create "I Care" cards to show that they are in the business of kindness. Encourage them to make the cards large if they like, and suggest that they design their own logos. (You may need to explain that a logo refers to the picture or symbol that appears on a business card.) Young people might also list a skill or service that they would be willing to provide, such as walking a dog, raking leaves, or sweeping a sidewalk.

For the sake of safety, kids should include only their first names—no last names, addresses, or telephone numbers. Instruct them to distribute their "I Care" cards only to adults they already know and trust. Remind the children that they should always seek parental permission before spending time with other adults.

When your group meets again later, ask young people to share how people responded to their cards.

EXTERNAL ASSETS: EMPOWERMENT

Children as Resources (Asset 8)

Focus
Children identify ways that they can help address larger social issues in the community.

Materials
☐ Photocopies of articles in newspapers or current events magazines that address social issues of particular relevance to children (e.g., hunger, child labor, antidiscrimination, disability rights, or second-hand smoke)
☐ Poster-size sheets of paper
☐ Markers, colored pencils, or crayons
☐ Resources about youth activism. One example is:
  ➤ *A Kid's Guide to Social Activism* by Barbara A. Lewis (Free Spirit Publishing, Inc., 1998)

Advance Preparations
Gather articles and draw a model "wanted" poster that solicits young people's involvement in a social issue.

Activity
Divide children into small groups and distribute the photocopied articles. Tell them they will be learning about needs and problems around the world to which children can contribute positive efforts that help make a difference. Ask each child to choose one article and read it silently. Then have members of each small group take turns summarizing the contents of their articles. Instruct the small groups to discuss the following questions:
  • What needs do you see in your neighborhood?
  • What kinds of problems do you see in the world?
  • If you could change one thing about your neighborhood or the world, what would it be?
  • What actions can young people take to help with problems they see in their neighborhood or world?
  • What stories do you know that are about children who have made a difference?

Stress that young people have the vision, creativity, and energy to become advocates for meaningful change. Share stories of children who studied a problem, decided to make a difference, and took action. (If you need examples, you can read success stories at the Youth Activism Project's Web site, which can be found at www. youthactivism.com.) Share this quote from anthropologist Margaret Mead:

Never doubt that a small group of thoughtful, committed citizens can change the world. Indeed, it's the only thing that ever has.

Ask young people to think of ways that they can work to change something that seems wrong or unfair. Encourage each child to choose an issue that is personally meaningful and to design a "wanted" poster to educate others about her or his chosen issue. Distribute paper and art supplies and share the poster you have designed with the group.

Explain that while "wanted" posters were first used to find criminals, the group will be designing posters to find helpers or invite people to take a certain action. For example, the poster could say canned goods or mittens are "wanted" for a food or clothing drive or that people are "wanted" to pick up litter. The poster may also "want" people to adopt a new attitude about an issue, such as greater tolerance for differences.

To help the young people choose their issue and design their posters, ask the following questions:
  • What issue most touches your heart and inspires you to take action?
  • What illustrations can you draw on the poster to capture peoples' hearts and attention?
  • How will your poster educate people about the issue you chose?
  • How will your poster inspire other people to care and take action?

Invite the children to share their posters with the large group. Ask them to choose one poster that has motivated them to take an action. Provide resources to guide participants in their efforts to help. Display the posters in a front hall, classroom, library, or other appropriate location.

Optional Variation
You might also invite your group to participate in one activity together, such as a canned food drive or a letter-writing campaign.

⑱ SECRET PALS

Service to Others (Asset 9)

Focus
Children learn the value of helping other people.

Materials
- ☐ Paper
- ☐ Pens or pencils
- ☐ Assorted art supplies to make a valentine, holiday card, or other small gift

Activity
Ask participants to recall times when people have done nice things for them. Encourage them to think of small gestures as well as larger efforts. Invite them to brainstorm a list of considerate or helpful things that they could do for other people.

At the conclusion of your discussion, ask each child to think of an adult in her or his life who deserves to be treated with extra kindness. Possibilities include teachers, youth program staff, coaches, extended family members, or neighbors. Explain that this adult will be a secret pal, and each participant will secretly do nice things for the adult he or she has chosen.

Have the children write the names of their chosen person at the top of a piece of paper. Then ask them to list some specific comments they can do, such as giving their pal compliments, volunteering to help the pal work on a project, or making small, anonymous gifts to leave for the pal.

Distribute the art supplies and let the children create a valentine, holiday card, or other small gift for their pal. Remind them not to sign their gift. Instruct the children to leave the gift for their secret pal and to also try to do some of the other ideas on their list.

At a later time, gather the group together for a follow-up discussion. You might begin with the following questions:
- What did you do for your secret pal?
- How did you feel when you did nice things for someone?
- How do you think your secret pal felt when you did these things?

Optional Variation
Have the children reveal their identities to their secret pals after giving their gift or trying one of their ideas. Instruct the young people to ask their secret pals how it felt to be appreciated. If possible, invite a secret pal to visit the group and share how it felt to receive secret special treatment.

EXTERNAL ASSETS: EMPOWERMENT

Service to Others (Asset 9)

Focus

Children have an opportunity to serve other people in the community.

Materials

☐ Short books, poems, and stories that have fairly wide appeal (at least one piece of text for each pair of youth)
☐ Pens or pencils
☐ Adhesive tape
☐ Scissors
☐ "Senior Story Hour Bookmark" Activity Sheet
☐ Transportation

Advance Preparations

Contact a nursing home or retirement community to schedule a visit with several residents. (You will need one senior resident for each pair of young people.) Arrange transportation for your young participants. Make photocopies of the "Senior Story Hour Bookmark" Activity Sheet to guide the children as they read to the senior residents.

Activity

Tell the children that the group will be visiting a nursing or retirement home to read to the residents. Explain that reading is a skill they have that they can share with others. Ask them to list the benefits of reading to the listener, such as enjoyment and learning new information.

Because young people may have concerns about interacting with elderly people or visiting a nursing or retirement home, talk about whether or not they have had previous experiences with older people. Acknowledge that because of health issues and an inability to care for themselves, many seniors need to live in a nursing or retirement home where they get assistance. Ask:

- Who are the oldest people who are a part of your life? Grandparents? Great-grandparents? Neighbors?
- What are some issues many older people have to deal with that younger people don't?

- Who has visited a nursing home or retirement home before? What can you tell the group about your experience?
- What questions do you have about nursing or retirement homes?

Point out that reading aloud to an older person might be different from reading aloud to someone younger. Being hard of hearing might be one issue that could come up. Encourage the children to think about other possible issues as well. Ask: *What do we need to do to show special respect while reading to these seniors?* Point out that the nursing home is where the residents live, so the children will be guests in the residents' home.

To address diverse abilities and ensure success for all children, divide the group into pairs in which there is a better reader and an improving reader. Be aware that some children may not be independent readers.

Invite each reading team to look through the books you have assembled. Ask them to choose a piece of writing that they would be interested in reading aloud to an older person.

Give them some time to practice reading loudly and clearly, and provide help with any unfamiliar pronunciations. Have the children plan how they will take turns reading with each other in pairs (e.g., every other page, every other chapter). Distribute a Senior Story Hour Bookmark to each child, and ask them to fill in their names and the reason they have chosen to read their particular selection aloud. Distribute scissors and tape so children can cut out their bookmarks and construct them. Review the "Tips for Readers" on the backside of the bookmark.

After the visit, conduct a follow-up discussion in which the children share their experiences reading to the residents. Reinforce the value of serving others. Ask the children to list some of the benefits they enjoyed, as well as benefits to the residents.

Senior Story Hour Bookmark

Cut out the bookmark and fold on the dotted line. Tape the open edge. Fill in the blanks and review the tips on the other side.

FOLD

Senior Story Hour Bookmark

Introduce yourself and ask the resident to introduce himself or herself.

My name is

_____.

What is your name?

I am sharing this book because

_____

_____

_____

_____.

Tips for Readers

• Take turns reading with your partner.

• Be sure to show any illustrations to your listener.

• Ask your listener to describe her or his favorite books: *What was your favorite book when you were growing up and why? What's your favorite book now and why?*

FOLD

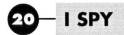

Safety (Asset 10)

Focus
Children examine their homes, neighborhoods, and schools to identify safety features, positive qualities, and areas that need improvement.

Materials
- ☐ Clipboard
- ☐ Safety helmet or construction hard hat
- ☐ Pens or pencils
- ☐ "I Spy" Activity Sheet

Activity
Ask for a volunteer who is interested in being a safety inspector. Give the volunteer the clipboard and the helmet or hard hat. Ask the volunteer to identify and examine one item or feature in the room to determine whether or not it appears to be safe. Possibilities include a sprinkler system, an office chair, or an electrical cord. Ask the inspector to explain what makes that feature safe or unsafe. A smoke detector would be an example of something safe, and a wobbly chair might be an example of something unsafe. Repeat with other volunteers.

Explain that in addition to safety tools or items, we need to practice safe behaviors. Discuss safe and unsafe behaviors that a person might observe in school, at the park, in the neighborhood, on the bus, and at home. Possibilities include wearing a seat belt or riding a bike with a helmet, or running in the halls or chewing gum while playing a sport. Ask group members to decide whether each behavior is safe or unsafe.

Distribute copies of the "I Spy" Activity Sheet to the children. Ask them to carry this checklist with them and record their observations as they walk around their school, neighborhood, and home.

When the group reconvenes, invite the young people to share their observations. Ask:
- What are some of the safe behaviors you noticed?
- What practices did you see that you would like to improve?
- What rules help keep you and others safe?
- What can you do to help make your school, neighborhood, and home as safe as possible? What would be safer for you *not* to do?

Optional Variation
Let older children act out the safety inspection for a group of younger children.

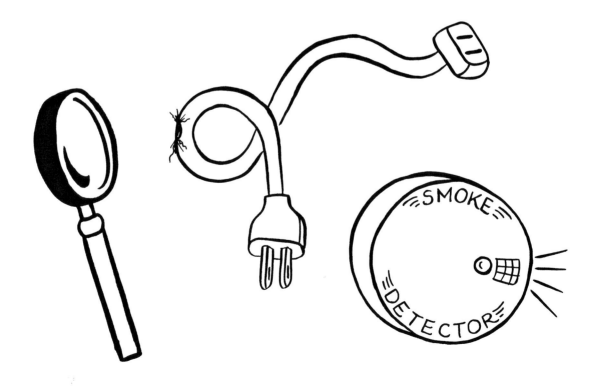

I Spy

Fill in things you see in your school, your neighborhood, or at home to complete the sentences below. Do not include the names of any people involved. Instead, think about your own actions and how you can behave to make the situation better.

I spy something that prevents accidents:

_____

I spy a broken item that could cause an accident:

_____

I spy something that prevents fires:

_____

I spy something that could start a fire:

_____

I spy a dangerous behavior:

_____

I spy a safe behavior:

_____

I spy a dangerous item in my home:

_____

I spy a safe item in my home:

_____

I spy a dangerous item in my school:

_____

I spy a safe item in my school:

_____

I spy something safe about my neighborhood:

_____

I spy something dangerous about my neighborhood:

_____

I spy one thing I can do to improve safety:

_____

Chapter 5

Boundaries and Expectations

Young people need the positive influence of peers and
adults who encourage them to be and do their best.
They also need clear rules about appropriate behavior
and consequences. The activities in this chapter allow
children to practice positive behaviors, learn the value
of rules, and understand that expectations are a way
of encouraging people to do their best.

EXTERNAL ASSETS: BOUNDARIES AND EXPECTATIONS

Family Boundaries (Asset 11)

Focus
Young people compare different kinds of family boundaries.

Materials
- ☐ Four large cans (such as coffee cans)
- ☐ Several sheets of paper
- ☐ Scissors

Advance Preparations
Make a list of topics that could involve family boundaries. Possible topics might include bedtime, friends, homework, sleepovers, clothing, expressing anger or sadness, watching TV, playing video games, disagreements with siblings, nutrition, movie ratings, curfew, or telephone calls. Make one photocopy of the list for each can, and cut the list into strips by items—or worms! Fill each can with all the strips from one list.

Activity
Divide the youth into four small groups. Introduce the phrase "a can of worms." Explain that "opening up a can of worms" refers to starting a discussion that has opposing views. Review guidelines for having a respectful discussion: taking turns listening, asking questions, and avoiding being judgmental or negative.

Invite the young people to open a can of worms by discussing family boundaries with each other. Explain that such a discussion might involve several differing ideas.

Stress the importance of creating a forum for exploring differences and understanding reasons for different preferences.

Give each team a can of worms. Have the young people take turns picking one strip of paper out of the can and reading it aloud. After reading the topic, each child in the group should explain what boundaries her or his parents or guardians have for that item. Participants should keep their slips of paper, and groups should continue to pass the can until all the strips of paper are drawn.

Ask the children to gather for a large-group discussion. Ask:

- What common boundaries do parents and guardians have for youth?
- Do you think most of these boundaries are okay? too strict? too lenient? Why do you feel that way?
- How do parents and guardians choose boundaries (e.g., on the basis of their own experiences, by discussing them with you, by discussing them with other people, based on what they think is "right" or acceptable)?
- How would your life be better if your parents or guardians didn't set boundaries? How would your life be worse?
- What would you tell a friend who had major disagreements with a parent or guardian about boundaries?

22 — LET'S MAKE A CHANGE

Family Boundaries (Asset 11)

Focus
Children practice negotiating boundary changes by role-playing.

Materials
☐ Scraps of scratch paper
☐ Pens or pencils
☐ Large can or jar

Activity
Begin with a large-group discussion of family rules. Invite the children to brainstorm a list of family boundaries in their homes. If they need help getting started, suggest the following topics:

- Restrictions on watching TV or playing computer and video games;
- Restrictions on how far from home children can go by themselves;
- Rules about baby-sitting or staying home alone; and
- Expectations for practicing manners at home or in public.

Distribute pencils and paper, and ask each participant to write down one example of a family boundary with which he or she is unhappy or disagrees. Ask them to specify how they would like to change the rule. Ask the children to fold the papers and put them in the can or jar.

Explain that members of the group will role-play a child asking a parent or guardian to revise the family rule. Suggest this is a good way to share ideas about how to negotiate change and to practice demonstrating the ability to handle greater responsibilities.

Be sure everyone understands that role playing involves pretending to be another person and acting out the situation. Ask for two volunteers to come to the front of the room: One will play the child and the other the parent or guardian. Draw an example from the jar and allow the children to act it out without interruption. After the pair has finished, ask:

- What did the young person say or do that was most effective in convincing the parent or guardian to change the family rule?
- What other ideas might the young person have tried?

Repeat the process until the group addresses all of the examples and everyone has had a chance to role-play.

23 — WHAT'S THE RULE?

School Boundaries (Asset 12)

Focus
Young participants understand how unclear rules can cause negative consequences.

Materials
☐ Paper
☐ Glue or tape
☐ Scissors

Activity
Begin by giving each child one piece of paper, a pair of scissors, and glue or tape. Give the children inconsistent and confusing directions. For example, say, *Fold the paper into quarters.* Wait, and then say, *Cut the paper into thirds.* Wait, and then say, *Attach one half of the paper to the other half.* If students ask for clarification, reply, *Please follow the rules.*

When the participants become somewhat frustrated by the activity, ask them to stop what they are doing. Give each person a new sheet of paper, and give a series of very specific rules. (Perhaps a small diagram, like a Japanese origami paper-folding graphic, could be added to the top of the page for extra visual support of oral instructions.) Ask the children to cut the paper into four long strips. Then, they should glue or tape one end of one strip to the other end of the same strip to create a circle. Continue with specific instructions for making a short paper chain. Demonstrate each step as you explain it.

Use the following questions to discuss the activity:

- How did you feel during the first part of the activity?
- What was good about having no rules for this project the first time you did it? What was bad about having no rules?
- How did you feel during the second part of the activity?
- What are some of the rules that you follow in school? What are the consequences when you don't follow the rules?
- How do the school's rules make you feel?
- How are rules helpful or important?

EXTERNAL ASSETS: BOUNDARIES AND EXPECTATIONS

Neighborhood Boundaries (Asset 13)

Focus

Young people gain an understanding of neighborhood boundaries by creating a board game.

Materials

- ☐ Poster-size sheets of card stock
- ☐ Crayons, markers, or colored pencils
- ☐ Scissors
- ☐ Paper
- ☐ "Good Neighbor Game" Activity Sheet

Activity

Divide participants into small groups. Distribute card stock and crayons, markers, or colored pencils. Explain that each group will create a board game to teach younger children different ways to show respect for neighbors and their property. Each group can begin by designing a traditional game board on a piece of card stock: a winding path with a "Start" and a "Finish" point, with about 20 spaces along the path.

Hand out the "Good Neighbor Game" Activity Sheet. Discuss the examples of boundaries on the sample game cards. Explain that for people to live together peacefully, they need to show respect for other people's property, pets, need for quiet, and so on.

Instruct the children to brainstorm examples of other neighborhood rules and boundaries in their small group. Have each child complete the activity sheet by creating additional game cards of positive and negative neighbor-hood situations. Each card should list a behavior as well as instructions for how to move on the game board (e.g., move ahead two spaces or back two spaces). Encourage each group to produce more positive situations than negative situations. Distribute scissors so that each group member can cut out her or his cards. Each group can collect every member's cards to create one deck. Also distribute paper so group members can design tokens for players to use as they move along the path on the game board.

Be sure to give your group some time to play the game. Have them take turns drawing a card and following the instructions to move forward or backward on the game board. Whoever reaches "Finish" first is the winner, or the "Good Neighbor." You may wish to use the game again at a subsequent meeting to allow for more playing time.

After playing the game, answer these questions:

- Why is it important to respect neighbors' homes and yards, pets, and other property?
- How does being thoughtful toward others in the neighborhood make it more likely that neighbors will be thoughtful and respectful of you?
- What does it mean to be a good neighbor? a bad neighbor?

Optional Variation

Invite younger siblings and other local children to visit and play the games.

The Good Neighbor Game

Use the boxes below to make game cards for the Good Neighbor Game. On each card, write one positive action or one negative action that a child could take in relating to her or his neighbors or neighborhood property. For a positive action, write down how many spaces forward the player can move. For a negative action, write down how many spaces backward the player must move. (See the three completed game cards below for examples.) Make sure that children younger than you will be able to relate to the situations. Cut along the dotted lines after you have labeled each card.

You asked permission before petting your neighbor's dog. **Move forward two spaces.**	You cut across a neighbor's lawn to get to your friend's house sooner. **Move backward three spaces.**	You turned down the volume on your stereo when your neighbor called to complain. **Move forward five spaces.**

Adult Role Models (Asset 14)

Focus

Participants identify the qualities of a positive, responsible adult role model.

Materials

☐ Sample trading cards of athletes, cartoon characters, fantasy characters, etc.

☐ Poster board or unlined index cards

☐ Scissors

☐ Crayons, markers, or colored pencils

Activity

Begin with a large-group discussion of role models. Explain that a positive adult role model is someone whom you want to be like as a grown-up. Children often see their parents and other family members as positive role models; sometimes, children want to be like other adults they know personally. Public figures can also act as role models for young people. Ask:

• Who are your role models?

• What makes a person a positive role model? What makes a person a negative role model?

• How important is it to know a role model personally?

Pass around the trading card samples and ask:

• What information do you see on the front and back of these cards?

• What qualities or statistics do the cards list?

• If you made a trading card about a positive role model, what information would you list on the back?

Invite participants to design oversized trading cards about their own positive role models using the index cards or poster board. Have each child draw a picture of the role model on one side and record identifying information about the role model on the other side. Invite them to share their trading cards and describe their choices first with a partner, then with the entire group.

26 — FOLLOW THE LEADER

Adult Role Models (Asset 14)

Focus
Young people identify character traits of a positive leader.

Materials
- ☐ Paper
- ☐ Pens or pencils
- ☐ "Follow the Leader" Activity Sheet

Activity
Begin by giving the children a series of instructions to divide them into small groups: Ask them to number off, direct the groups to meet in various areas of the room, and request that the children move quietly into their small group. Observe what you have done and what they have done: You have given instructions, and they have followed them.

Explain that leaders are people who guide groups of people to do certain things and model behaviors for the group. Acknowledge that there can be positive leaders and negative leaders, but say that the group will be focusing today on the qualities that make a positive leader one type of role model. Ask participants to brainstorm the traits of a positive leader. Write them where the group can see their responses.

Distribute paper and pencils. Ask each young person, working privately, to write the name of an adult who is a leader in her or his life at the top of a piece of paper. Explain that they are welcome to choose any person who is a model of good leadership. Their choices might include someone they know personally such as a teacher, coach, or family member, or they may choose a public figure such as a politician, artist, or athlete.

Below the leader's name, ask each participant to list five positive qualities that make the person a good leader. When young people are finished writing their lists, ask the children to take turns sharing in their small group their list of positive qualities. Ask them to identify which qualities occurred most frequently.

Distribute the "Follow the Leader" Activity Sheet. Ask each participant to list the qualities that occurred most frequently in their small group in the "Positive Leadership Quality" column. In the "Action" column, have them describe specific actions that demonstrate each trait. In the column labeled "Message," ask children to write dialogue statements to identify things a person might say if he or she possessed that positive leadership trait. Review the example on the activity sheet.

Invite the participants to take turns being the leader of their small group. Have them practice using the messages and actions they have identified to lead the group to put away their chairs at the end of the activity or to take some other responsible action.

Optional Variation
Calculate which leadership qualities occur most frequently and graph their frequency.

Follow the Leader

In the first column, list five positive leadership qualities that are most important for being a good leader. In the other two columns, list actions and messages that demonstrate each leadership quality.

Positive Leadership Quality	Action	Message
Communication	A good leader talks to many people and listens to ideas before making decisions.	"I would like to tell you about a problem, and I would like to hear what you think about it."

27 — LINK TAG

Positive Peer Influence (Asset 15)

Focus
Children see how working together with responsible peers can achieve positive results.

Materials
☐ A gym, outdoor area, or other space for running

Activity
Explain that the group is going to play a form of Tag. Set boundaries for the playing area (not too large), as well as an out-of-bounds area. Choose two people to be "It." Explain that the "It" people will hold hands as they chase the others, and as they tag people, the tagged people should join hands with the "It" people. Remind the children to play safely and not to drag or pull someone down if the person is a slower runner. Begin the game.

As the "It" chain grows longer, it will become harder for the chased players to dodge the expanding "It" chain without stepping out of bounds. Replay the game a few times with a new "It" pair each time. Afterward, invite the children to reflect on their experiences by asking:
- How hard was it to avoid being tagged by two people? by five people? by eight people?
- Was it easier to tag people when you were part of a two-person "It" chain or when you were part of a ten-person "It" chain? Why?
- What were the advantages of a long "It" chain? What were the disadvantages?

Expand the discussion to address issues of peer cooperation and influence. Ask:
- What does the word *peer* mean? Who are your peers?
- How does it feel to be part of a group of peers working together?
- How do your peers influence your decisions? What kind of advice do they give you?
- How can you respond if a peer tells you to do something dangerous?
- How can you identify the positive "links" in your friendship "chains" who help you make good decisions?

End the discussion by stressing that each of us can be a positive influence in the lives of our friends and peers. Remind children that working together can often achieve more positive results than working alone.

28 — PEER DOWN THE ROAD

Positive Peer Influence (Asset 15)

Focus
Young people interview adults to find out facts about life-long friendships.

Materials
☐ Paper and pencils
☐ Crayons, markers, or colored pencils
☐ "Peer Down the Road" Activity Sheet

Activity
Divide the young people into pairs. Instruct them to write down questions they could ask each other to learn what makes a good friend, as well as what makes a friendship last. Possible questions might include:
- How did you meet your friends?
- Which of your friendships have lasted a long time?
- Why do you think they have?
- What qualities do you most enjoy in your friends?
- What makes a friend trustworthy?
- How do you show your friends that you care?

Instruct the pairs of children to interview each other and record the answers.

Invite the children to collect data about long-term friendships by using their questions to interview parents or guardians, teachers, or other adults. Once the young people have interviewed adults, have a large-group discussion and ask:
- Did anyone interview an adult who still has a friend from childhood?
- How did adults keep their long-term friendships?
- What qualities do long-lasting friendships have in common?
- How will you use this information as you choose your own friends?

Distribute the "Peer Down the Road" Activity Sheet. Invite the children to draw cartoons that illustrate scenes from a current friendship and then "peer down the road" to imagine what that friendship might look like in the future.

Optional Variation
Bind the cartoons together to make a "friendship book" to present to younger children.

Peer Down the Road

Think about your friends, and choose one friendship that you think will last a lifetime. In the cartoon strip below, illustrate your friendship. In the top three squares, draw the story of how you became friends. In the bottom three squares, draw a story of what you think your friendship will be like when you are adults.

How We Became Friends

Our Friendship Down the Road

High Expectations (Asset 16)

Focus

Young people describe expectations for themselves and make predictions about their future selves.

Materials

☐ One lidded jar or coffee can per participant

☐ Pencils or pens

☐ "Time Capsule" Activity Sheet

Activity

Share the following quote from professional basketball player Michael Jordan:

> *You have to expect things of yourself before you*
> *do them.*

Invite young people to share their thoughts and feelings about Michael Jordan's statement. Define an expectation as setting a goal of something you would like to do or a way you would like to be in the future. Other ways to describe an expectation are as a hope or as an intention.

Distribute the "Time Capsule" Activity Sheet and the lidded jars or coffee cans. Explain that each child will make a time capsule that contains her or his personal expectations. Give time for each child to complete the activ-ity sheet, and suggest that the activity sheet be the first item in the time capsule.

Invite group members to suggest other items they could place in the time capsule that would illustrate their expectations for themselves. Possible ideas include:

- Articles or newspaper clippings about issues that are important to them;
- Postcards of places around the world that they would like to visit;
- Samples of schoolwork from favorite subjects;
- Pictures of role models, family members, or friends who have achieved important goals; and
- Objects from hobbies or skills that the children hope to explore further.

Encourage participants to keep their time capsules hidden in a safe place. Invite them to revisit their time capsules and reread their expectations later in life to see how their goals change over the years.

Optional Variation

If you work with the same group of kids for a full year, keep the capsules and invite the children to open the capsules at the end of the year.

Time Capsule

Looking into the future, think about your goals for yourself as an adult. Fill in the time capsules with words and drawings of your answers.

My Name: _____ Today's Date: _____

A job I might like to have:

Artistic or musical talents I hope to develop:

A hobby I might enjoy:

A place I plan to travel:

My best qualities as a person:

My strongest skills:

High Expectations (Asset 16)

Focus
Young people identify how adults can communicate high expectations in caring ways.

Materials
☐ Pens or pencils
☐ "Chilled, Grilled, or Toasted?" Activity Sheet

Activity
Ask for a volunteer to pretend to be a kid coming home from school. Instruct the rest of the group to pretend to be the parents or guardians asking all sorts of questions. Sample questions might include:
- How much homework do you have?
- Did you score in the game today?
- Where is my newspaper?
- Did you eat your lunch?
- Will you please be quiet?
- Did you learn anything interesting today?
- Why don't you read a book instead of watching TV?

Ask the volunteer how the steady stream of questions made her or him feel. Ask the group to discuss which questions seemed too worried or harsh, which questions seemed caring and interested, and which questions made it sound like the parent or guardian didn't care about the young person or wasn't paying attention. Remind participants that it is fine if they have different opinions about which questions fall into which categories.

Suggest that our parents' or guardians' questions and expectations are a little bit like the heat from a stove. You might use a speech like this one:

If our parents don't ask about our talents and our efforts, we might feel ignored, like they didn't even turn on the stove. This can leave us feeling "chilled." If they ask us too many questions and get too worried, we might feel pressured, like they turned the stove up too high. This can make us feel "grilled" by the things they say. We want our parents to care about us and expect us to do our best, but we might get frustrated if we feel like they expect too much. Instead of feeling chilled or grilled, we want to feel pleasantly cheered on, or "toasted."

Ask group members to share how they feel when their parents or guardians ask questions:
- How do you feel when your parents do not talk to you about school or other activities?
- What questions do you *not* want to hear?
- What questions *do* you want to hear?

Distribute the "Chilled, Grilled, or Toasted?" Activity Sheet. Invite participants to list some of the things their parents have said to them. Ask young people to check one of the boxes next to each comment or question to indicate how it makes them feel. Invite them to take their lists home and discuss this concept with their parents or guardians, using the discussion topics at the bottom of the activity sheet.

Chilled, Grilled, or Toasted?

Use this activity sheet to talk with your parents or guardians about how their questions and comments make you feel. In the column on the left, list some of the things that your parents or guardians have said to you. Check the box to indicate whether each comment or question makes you feel "chilled" (ignored), "grilled" (overly pressured), or "toasted" (encouraged).

Question or Comment from My Parent or Guardian	Chilled	Grilled	Toasted

Use the discussion topics below to talk to your parents or guardians about the way their words make you feel.

It makes me feel like you don't care about me when you don't talk to me about this school subject, hobby, or activity: _____

It makes me feel nervous and pressured when you expect me to do better in this school subject, hobby, or activity: _____

It makes me feel good when you talk to me and expect me to do my best in this school subject, hobby, or activity: _____

These are some things that I would like to hear you say to me to help me do my best:

_____

Chapter 6

Constructive Use of Time

Children thrive when they spend their time in a
variety of creative and educational endeavors. The activities
in this chapter help young people build on their current
interests as well as explore new pursuits.

Creative Activities (Asset 17)

Focus

Participants use creativity to turn a favorite story into a musical play.

Materials

☐ Audio or video samples from musical plays or movies that are based on children's literature. For example:
  ➤ *Willy Wonka and the Chocolate Factory* based on the book *Charlie and the Chocolate Factory* by Roald Dahl
  ➤ *Oliver!* based on *Oliver Twist* by Charles Dickens
  ➤ *The Wizard of Oz* based on *The Wizard of Oz* by L. Frank Baum

☐ Paper

☐ Pens or pencils

Activity

Play selections from the musicals and encourage the children to sing along if they know the songs. Ask them if they can identify the musical. Explain that many musicals are based on books. Ask the children if they know the books upon which the musicals they are listening to are based. If possible, identify the section of the book that forms the basis for each song, and invite volunteers to read that section aloud. Discuss ways in which the books and songs are different. Ask: *What is special about telling a story through music?*

As a group, brainstorm a list of familiar stories or books that have not already been made into musical plays or films. Narrow the list down to a few popular choices, and have the young people vote on one story that they would like to make into a musical play. Ask a volunteer to summarize the story for anyone who is not familiar with it.

Ask the group to think about the plot of the story and determine three topics for songs. Use these questions to identify good song topics:
  • How would you introduce the characters?
  • What is the most important thing that happens in the middle of the story?
  • What is the grand finale that ends the story?

If, for example, the children decide they would like to make a musical for younger children based on the story *The Very Hungry Caterpillar* by Eric Carle, they might introduce their main character with a song called "I Am a Hungry Caterpillar." They might tell what goes on in the middle of the story with a song called, "Let Me Tell You about All the Stuff I Ate," and end with the grand finale, "Now I'm a Butterfly!"

Divide the young people into three groups, and assign each group to write lyrics for one song in the musical. If possible, give each group a private space where they can practice their song without distracting the other groups. Encourage participants to create their own melodies, but if they become frustrated, suggest that they write new lyrics for familiar melodies, such as "Twinkle, Twinkle, Little Star" or "Zip-A-Dee-Doo-Dah."

Reunite the three groups for a chronological performance of the songs. Let each group sing for the other two groups, and afterward ask participants to reflect on how well the three songs worked together to tell the story.

Optional Variation

Use a bag of props to enhance the performance. If you play an instrument, invite the kids to write new lyrics to songs you can play. If time and resources permit, develop the three songs into a full version of the musical with costumes and a set. The group could perform the musical for parents or guardians, younger children, or senior citizens.

Creative Activities (Asset 17)

Focus

Children participate in a service project that promotes interest in visual art.

Materials

- ☐ Paper
- ☐ Scissors
- ☐ Adhesive tape or glue
- ☐ Paints and brushes
- ☐ Crayons, markers, colored pencils, and/or chalk
- ☐ Clay or other materials for sculptures
- ☐ Telephone and directory
- ☐ Transportation

Advance Preparations

Call several community organizations that your group could realistically work with, and try to find at least one place that will accept and display donated artwork from the children. If possible, plan a time when your group of artists can visit and present their donation or hold an art opening or reception. If the organization cannot accommodate your group in person, make preparations to drop off a package with a letter and photograph from your group.

Activity

Invite young people to identify places in their community that would benefit from a donation of artwork. Some examples might include a public library, a homeless shelter, a day-care center, or a hospital. In a rural area, participants may consider nearby schools or stores. In an urban area, they may think of community centers and government buildings. Discuss the possibilities as a group and list several locations where participants would like to see artwork displayed.

Share with participants the results of your earlier contacts with community organizations. Discuss any contingencies of space available, possible themes, weather limitations, the possibility of an art opening, and any other factors that may have come up in your preparatory conversations. Distribute art supplies and give young people time to create paintings, drawings, and sculptures to give away to a willing organization.

At a follow-up meeting, ask the young people how they felt their artistic efforts were received:

- How did it feel to make art for someone who really wanted your efforts?
- What did you learn from the experience?
- What would you do differently next time? keep the same?
- Do you see yourself as an artist? Why or why not?

Child Programs (Asset 18)

Focus
Young people learn about some of the children's programs available in their community.

Materials
☐ Tables or desks arranged for small groups
☐ Paper
☐ Pens or pencils
☐ "Community Program Fair" Activity Sheet

Advance Preparations
Contact leaders of several youth programs in your community who are interested in recruiting participants and invite them to meet with your group. Try for a diverse selection of program types, including at least one athletic program and one arts program. Make sure that the selected programs are inexpensive; also request information about scholarship options.

Ask leaders to plan to speak for a few minutes to the whole group of children, giving brief descriptions of their programs. Explain that they will also have the opportunity to give more detailed information in smaller groups. Encourage the program representatives to bring literature, photos, audiovisual equipment and props, or plan brief activities to share with prospective program attendees.

Also notify parents and guardians that their children will be participating in a child program fair that will introduce them to enrichment activities they might want to pursue. You may wish to invite parents and guardians to attend the program fair.

Activity
Before the day of the program fair, explain the rotation format of the fair to everyone. (See below for details.) Also stress the value of participating in activities. Ask:
- Which of your skills or talents would you like to develop further?
- Do you have a skill you would like to work on or one you wish you had?

In a large group on the day of the program fair, introduce each program leader to the children and their parents or guardians. Have each leader share a brief description of the program activities.

After introductions, assign each group leader to a station in the room. Divide participants with their parents and guardians evenly among the stations and tell them they will have about five minutes at each station. (Adjust according to the number of program leaders and your own time constraints.)

Give every young person a "Community Program Fair" Activity Sheet to fill out as they visit each station. Encourage youth to ask questions about each program and to look at any materials or samples that the leaders have provided.

When five minutes have passed, announce that participants should rotate clockwise to the next program station. Repeat until every young person has visited every program station. Make sure that children who do not have parents or guardians in attendance obtain a brochure about the program that most interests them so they have contact information to take home.

When your group gets together next, check in with the kids. Discuss what steps they have taken to participate in a program.

Community Program Fair

As you visit with different program leaders at the Community Program Fair, fill in this form to help you decide which programs interest you the most.

What is the name of the program?	What would I do in the program?	What would I learn?	Does this program interest me?	What do my parents or guardians need to know?*

*For example, registration deadline, location, time, cost, and materials.

Which programs interest me the most? Why? _____

_____

What action do I need to take to get involved with these programs? _____

_____

EXTERNAL ASSETS: CONSTRUCTIVE USE OF TIME

Religious Community (Asset 19)

Focus
Children learn about the traditions youth follow for entry into adulthood in a variety of faith communities.

Materials
☐ Paper
☐ Pens or pencils

Advance Preparations
Invite representatives from several religious organizations to visit your group to speak about how their faith communities mark the transition from childhood to adulthood. Contact representatives from diverse traditions, and include both men and women. Stress that you would like the representatives to speak about traditions and customs rather than religious belief systems.

Also notify parents and guardians that their children will attend a program that will expose them to people of differing faith backgrounds. Consider inviting parents and guardians to attend the program.

Activity
Before your guest speakers join the group, explain to the children that representatives from several faith communities will be visiting. Encourage the young people to think about their own involvement with a faith community. Use these questions to guide your discussion:
* Are you involved with a faith community? a faith-based youth group? a religion class?
* In your faith communities, what kinds of ceremonies do young people go through to show that they are becoming adults?

Distribute paper and pencils and ask the group to brainstorm a list of questions to ask the guest speakers. Stress the need for tolerance of different religious traditions. Ask the children to practice their questions aloud, speaking slowly and clearly so the whole group can hear. Make sure the children understand that they need to speak to the religious representatives respectfully.

When the speakers arrive, invite each religious representative to speak briefly about the rite of passage into adulthood in her or his tradition. Invite young people to take turns asking the questions they have prepared. Keep the focus on traditions and customs rather than doctrine.

Time at Home (Asset 20)

Focus
Children analyze how they use their time.

Materials
☐ Pens or pencils
☐ "Where Does the Time Go?" Activity Sheet

Activity
Divide the young people into pairs. Instruct the children to ask each other: *What's one thing that's possible for you to do tomorrow that you'd really like to do?* Invite the young people to share their predictions with their partner about how much time they will actually spend the next day eating, sleeping, in school, watching television or playing video games, playing with friends, doing homework, reading, participating in a youth program, or spending time with family and friends.

Distribute the "Where Does the Time Go?" Activity Sheet and pens or pencils. In the first column, ask young people to record brief predictions about what they will do during each waking hour of the day. Instruct the young people to use the activity sheet the next day to record the ways that they actually spent their time. Emphasize that it is absolutely fine if their predictions do not match their results.

During a later meeting, ask participants to share their completed activity sheets with their partners and report on how they actually spent their time. Did they do the one thing they most wanted to do? Invite the pairs to discuss their thoughts about how to spend time. Suggest questions such as:
* What surprised you about how you actually spent your time?
* What different decisions might you make about how you spend time?
* What's good about how you spend your time now? What might you like to change?
* How might you benefit from spending your time differently?

Invite volunteers to share their results and to discuss ideas for spending meaningful time at home. Encourage them to look at their activity sheets and identify areas where they might reorganize their time and reach a healthy balance of activities. End by suggesting each participant decide on one action step he or she can take the next day to spend time in a more meaningful way.

Where Does the Time Go?

In the first column, make predictions about what you think you will be doing at each hour during the day tomorrow. In the second column, keep track of how you actually spend your time. Remember that it is fine if your activities do not match your predictions.

Time	Prediction	Actual Activities
8:00 A.M.		
9:00 A.M.		
10:00 A.M.		
11:00 A.M.		
12:00 P.M.		
1:00 P.M.		
2:00 P.M.		
3:00 P.M.		
4:00 P.M.		
5:00 P.M.		
6:00 P.M.		
7:00 P.M.		
8:00 P.M.		

Time at Home (Asset 20)

Focus
Children identify enjoyable activities they can engage in at home.

Materials
- [ ] Pens or pencils
- [ ] "Hobby Day" Activity Sheet

Advance Preparations
Ask the children to bring in an object that represents a hobby they enjoy at home, such as a violin, jigsaw puzzle, fish food for their fish, baseball glove, chemistry set, coin collection, yo-yo, or model airplane. Explain that watching TV does not count as a hobby.

Activity
Divide the children into small groups and invite them to share their hobbies with each other. Have them explain the hobby and, if possible, demonstrate it. Ask the group members to decide in what category the hobby fits: *Is it artistic? scientific? a sport? related to animals? something they collect?* Some hobbies, such as horseback riding, might fall into more than one category.

Distribute the "Hobby Day" Activity Sheet. Ask young people to fill in the blanks, but let them know it is okay to leave items blank. Encourage the participants to share with their small group one hobby they might like to pursue. Acknowledge that some hobbies, such as horseback riding or photography, might be difficult to pursue because of cost. But stress that many hobbies, such as learning to do tricks with a yo-yo, can be very inexpensive.

Hobby Day

Fill in the blanks below to explore your hobbies at home.

When I am home, I usually spend my time: _____

_____.

My current artistic hobby is: _____

_____.

An artistic hobby that I would like to begin is: _____

_____.

My current scientific hobby is: _____.

_____

A scientific hobby that I would like to begin is: _____.

_____

One collection I have is: _____.

_____

One thing I would like to begin collecting is: _____.

_____

A sport I enjoy is: _____.

Another sport I would like to learn is: _____.

An animal-related hobby I have is: _____.

An animal-related hobby I would like to begin is: _____.

The new hobby that I am most interested in pursuing during my time
at home is: _____.

One person who might be willing to help me is: _____.

One action I can take to get going on this hobby is: _____.

_____

By this date: _____, I will take this action so I can share what happened.

PART 3

Internal Assets

Commitment to Learning

It's important for children to be excited about learning
inside and outside of school. The activities in this chapter
teach young people to take pride in their work and
offer fun ways to make learning meaningful.

Achievement Motivation (Asset 21)

Focus

Each participant learns one special word chosen to inspire individual achievement.

Materials

- ☐ Dictionaries
- ☐ Thesauruses
- ☐ Pens or pencils
- ☐ "My Special Word" Activity Sheet

Advance Preparations

Select one special word for each young person in the group, being careful that the words are not judgmental or hurtful in any way. Try to choose words that are challenging, but not too advanced for the vocabulary level of your group. If possible, select a word that is especially appropriate for each individual. Possible words include *honest, confident, generous, persistent, ambitious, creative, compassionate, visionary, talented, intelligent,* and *brave.* On each child's copy of the "My Special Word" Activity Sheet, fill in that child's name and special word.

Activity

Distribute the "My Special Word" Activity Sheet to the children. Tell them:

On this sheet of paper, you will find your special word. This might be a familiar word, or it might be a word that you have never heard. I would like you to learn about this word and consider what it means to you personally. You might already experience this word in your own daily life and actions, or you might like to explore this word and use it to think about yourself.

Give the young people time to work independently to use the dictionaries and thesauruses to learn more about their word. Instruct them to complete the statements on the activity sheet. Invite the young people to keep the activity sheet with their special word in a private place and revisit it during the next several months.

Optional Variation

If your group meets regularly, give each participant a new word every month.

My Special Word

You've been given a special word to inspire you to do your very best. Fill in the blanks to help you learn more about what your word means and how to use your word in your life. Use the back of this page to draw a picture that illustrates your word.

My name is: _____.

My special word is: _____.

My word means: _____

_____.

My word makes me think about: _____

_____.

Here is a sentence that uses my special word: _____

_____.

This is something I have already done that is an example

of my word: _____

_____.

This is something I can do during the next week that will

be an example of my word: _____

_____

_____.

Learning Engagement (Asset 22)

Focus
Participants identify ideas that inspire them to learn on their own.

Materials
☐ Pens or pencils
☐ "Wonderstorms" Activity Sheet

Advance Preparations
Make a poster showing your own "wonderstorm."

Activity
Explain to the large group that a *wonderstorm* is a question that fills you with a sense of wonder and curiosity. Share the poster showing your own "wonderstorm." Examples might include:

- Why does one person's yawn make another person yawn?
- How does music come from a round plastic-and-aluminum disc?
- Why do squirrels chase each other?
- How do babies figure out how to walk?
- How do trees know to grow leaves after winter?
- How do people in deserts live with so little water?

Distribute the "Wonderstorms" Activity Sheet and invite young people to list questions or ideas that fill them with wonder. Use the following questions to help kids generate their own ideas:

- If you were a scientist, what topics would you research?
- If you could travel anywhere in the world, which countries would you visit?
- What about our world fills you with a sense of wonder?

Give participants time to complete the activity sheet. Divide them into sharing groups so each person can describe her or his "wonderstorm." Discuss ways that kids can investigate and learn more about topics that interest them.

Optional Variation
Conclude the activity with a trip to a library and give kids time to search for information about their "wonderstorms."

Wonderstorms

A wonderstorm is a question that fills you with a sense of wonder. Use the statements below to help you discover your own "wonderstorms." Try to phrase your "wonderstorms" as questions.

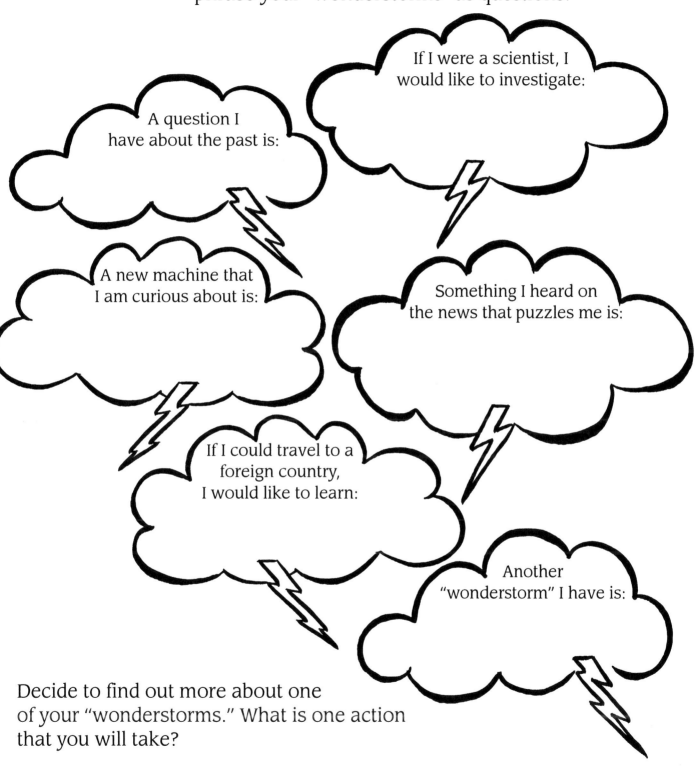

If I were a scientist, I would like to investigate:

A question I have about the past is:

A new machine that I am curious about is:

Something I heard on the news that puzzles me is:

If I could travel to a foreign country, I would like to learn:

Another "wonderstorm" I have is:

Decide to find out more about one of your "wonderstorms." What is one action that you will take?

Homework (Asset 23)

Focus

Young people develop strategies for successfully managing their homework responsibilities.

Materials

☐ Poems, stories, or audio stories about homework. Possible examples include:
  ➤ "Homework! Oh, Homework!" a poem by Jack Prelutsky, from *The New Kid on the Block* (Greenwillow Books, 1990)
  ➤ "Zanzibar," a story on tape by Bill Harley, from *Cool in School* (Round River Records, 1987)
☐ Pens and pencils
☐ Colored pencils, markers, or crayons
☐ "Mission Possible" Activity Sheet

Activity

Read your homework poem or story aloud to the children. Afterward, adopt a serious tone and give the following speech:

This may sound like a simple poem or story, but it is actually a secret assignment from a government agency. Apparently there are some young people who have a hard time with their homework. Your mission as a secret agent is to train yourself and other students to get homework done and to have fun doing it!

Explain that you will be dividing the "agents" into teams to focus on different parts of this challenge. You may choose your own topics, or you may use the team names below. Give participants time to discuss their topics in teams, and then ask teams to report back to the larger group. After all of the teams have reported their strategies, ask volunteers to share homework success stories.

Conclude the activity with the "Mission Possible" Activity Sheet. Ask young people to think of this worksheet as a personal plan for continuing work as a secret homework agent.

TEAM NAMES

Language Specialists
Study the word *homework* and try to come up with a more positive name for it. (Examples are "Think Time," "Learning Invitations," or "Brain Exercises.") Add slogans or code phrases to describe the names you generate.

Headquarters Operations
Create a homework headquarters where an agent will be excited to do work. What will this space look like? How will you make it inviting and comfortable for the agents who work there?

Trainers and Equipment Specialists
What talents, gadgets, and skills would an excellent homework agent have? How could he or she practice these skills?

Success Supervisors
When your agents do a good job with their homework, how will you reward them? How will you make their jobs fun?

Mission Possible

You have accepted your new job as a secret homework agent. Answer the following questions to explain how you will meet the homework challenge.

My more positive code name for *homework* is:

_____

I am training myself to have these important study

skills: _____

_____

_____

For maximum homework success, the special features I have installed in

my homework headquarters are: _____

_____

_____

The reward I give myself when I complete my homework is: _____

_____

_____

Bonding to Adults at School (Asset 24)

Focus

Children recognize and appreciate all of the adults who contribute to the success of their school.

Materials

☐ Paper
☐ Pens or pencils

Activity

Invite the young people to develop a list of all the adults who are somehow involved with their school. Encourage them to think beyond teachers. Other adults might include lunchroom staff, bus drivers, custodians, counselors, fine arts directors, volunteers, parents and guardians, librarians, receptionists, coaches, nurses, aides, principals and superintendents, and school board members.

Divide young people into small groups, and give each group one or two of the categories of adults that they have identified. Ask the groups to answer the following questions for each category of adults:

• How do these adults make the school a better place?
• Have you ever thanked these adults for their contributions?
• If you were to plan an Appreciation Day for this group of adults, what could you do to show your thanks?

Help students generate ideas that include and acknowledge *all* staff members in the school, not only the high-profile or more popular individuals. Encourage students to develop their ideas for an Appreciation Day and submit their proposals to the school's administration. Follow up with the administration to help the students implement their ideas.

INTERNAL ASSETS: COMMITMENT TO LEARNING

Reading for Pleasure (Asset 25)

Focus
Children explore ways to increase their enjoyment of reading.

Materials
☐ Pens or pencils
☐ Chalkboard or chart paper
☐ "Take Me to Your Reader Survey" Activity Sheet

Activity
Introduce yourself as an alien from another planet. Explain that you have just arrived on Earth, and you wish to learn more about this human activity called *reading*. Request that group members help you gather information to take back to your home planet.

Divide the children into small groups to discuss how they feel about reading. Ask them to answer the following questions:

- Would you rather read a book, a magazine, or a comic strip?
- Would you rather read in a rocking chair, under a shade tree, or under the covers in bed?
- In school, would you rather read at a desk, on a rug, on pillows, or in a reclining chair?
- After you read a good book, would you rather write your thoughts in a journal, talk about the adventures with a friend, or create a work of art inspired by the story?
- Would you rather watch television, play a video game, or read a good book?

Ask groups to share their responses with the larger group.

Distribute the "Take Me to Your Reader Survey" Activity Sheet. Invite participants to interview family, friends, students, school personnel, and neighbors to explore attitudes about reading. Participants should record responses with checks or tally marks.

During a later meeting, compile survey results and write totals on a chalkboard or on chart paper. Ask participants to think about how they can use the data to inspire people to become lifelong readers. Divide into small groups, and ask each group to consider one of the following questions:

- Based on the data collected, how can we create spaces that inspire reading in schools? in our homes? in our libraries?
- What reading materials could a library collect to meet the interests of people in our community?
- What kinds of story-sharing projects could we initiate?

Invite small groups to share ideas with the larger group. Encourage young people to share their data with parents and guardians, teachers, and librarians.

Optional Variation
Invite a bookseller or librarian to talk about how they select a wide variety of books to meet the interests of diverse readers.

Take Me to Your Reader Survey

To better understand the reading habits of earthlings, ask five earthlings to answer the following questions. Place a check or tally mark next to each earthling's answer. You may have more than one tally mark next to an answer if people have the same opinions.

1. Where do you prefer to read?
___ Under blankets in bed
___ In a library
___ At school
___ Under a shady tree
___ On the couch in my living room
___ Other:_____

2. Which would you rather read?
___ The newspaper
___ A comic book
___ A book of poetry
___ A science book
___ A funny story
___ A true story about a real person
___ Other:_____

3. Which would you rather receive as a gift?
___ A gift certificate to a bookstore
___ A subscription to *TV Guide*
___ A set of encyclopedias
___ A complete set of books by an author I like
___ A dictionary or thesaurus
___ A subscription to the following magazine:_____

4. What kind of fiction (imaginary stories) do you most like to read?
___ Action stories
___ Sad stories
___ Romantic stories
___ Funny stories
___ Mystery stories
___ Other:_____

5. What kind of nonfiction (true stories) do you most like to read?
___ Newspapers and current events magazines
___ Biographies
___ How-to books
___ Science and nature books
___ History books
___ Other:_____

INTERNAL ASSETS: COMMITMENT TO LEARNING

Reading for Pleasure (Asset 25)

Focus
Young people share with others the books that are exciting and special to them.

Materials
- ☐ Sample of a book you cherish
- ☐ Paper
- ☐ Crayons, markers, or colored pencils
- ☐ Scissors

Advance Preparations
Select an exciting or interesting excerpt or chapter of a book that is special to you. Create a sign, bookmark, or book jacket that would help you "sell" your book.

Activity
Introduce yourself as a traveling book salesperson. Explain that you are stopping by to visit a group of customers to tell them about one of your favorite books. Read aloud a selection from the book. Then, describe "selling points" to entice the children to continue reading your book. Hint at interesting events that happen later in

the book or fascinating characters they might want to meet.

Ask each young person to think about a favorite book that he or she has read for fun and would like to promote. Invite them to approach this task as a salesperson. Use these questions to help them think about how to "market" their books:
- What makes this book one of your favorites?
- Who are your favorite characters in the book?
- What information might convince potential readers to select your book?
- What are your favorite lines or scenes from the story?
- How did this book change the way you think?
- What clues can you give about exciting things that happen in the book?

Suggest that it is important not to give away the ending of the book. Remind them that if a salesperson gives everything away, there will be nothing left to buy!

Invite participants to create signs, bookmarks, or book covers to advertise the book to other readers. (Young people may not be familiar with the term *book jacket,* so you should show them an example and read the information that appears on the book jacket.) Suggest that they use catchy phrases and slogans the way an advertiser might. Display books and promotional materials on a special shelf where young people can read each other's recommendations. If possible, create the display during a special "Book Week" at a school or library.

Optional Variation
Invite each kid to dress as a favorite character from her or his favorite book. Let each person promote her or his book from the character's point of view.

Chapter 8

Positive Values

Positive values give children the confidence to make responsible decisions. These activities allow young people to explore their beliefs and identify healthy, empathetic choices.

Caring (Asset 26)

Focus
Children and their families work together to help others.

Materials
- ☐ Large basket with enough cookies, stickers, or similar items to distribute one to each group member
- ☐ Pens or pencils
- ☐ Colored pencils, markers, or crayons
- ☐ "Care Package" Activity Sheet

Advance Preparations
Create a large care package so that every member of the group can receive one of each item. Include inexpensive items such as cookies and stickers.

Activity
Begin by telling the young people that you care about them: In fact, you care so much for them that you want to *show* them you care for them. Explain that you have created a care package for the group. Ask a volunteer to describe a care package. Make sure the children understand these features of a care package:

- It typically arrives as a surprise;
- It usually contains more than one item;
- Items can be inexpensive or, even better, homemade;
- Items can be practical, fun, or inspirational;
- Items show caring for the person who receives it; or
- The recipient is usually someone special who is far away from home or having a difficult time.

Invite the children forward to receive their care package items. Ask them: *How does it feel to receive an unexpected present?*

Suggest that the young people think about creating a care package to give to someone special. Direct the participants to break into small groups to discuss the following:

- In what situations might someone really appreciate a care package?
- To whom would you like to send a care package?
- What practical items, messages, or homemade gifts might you include in your care package?

Distribute the "Care Package" Activity Sheet along with pencils and art supplies. Suggest that the children talk with their parents and guardians to decide to whom they might send a care package. Invite them to think about the contents they might include.

Care Package

Write the name of the person to whom you would like to send a care package as well as your name on the gift tag. Draw pictures of the things you will put in your care package. Talk to your parents or guardians about delivering your care package to this special person.

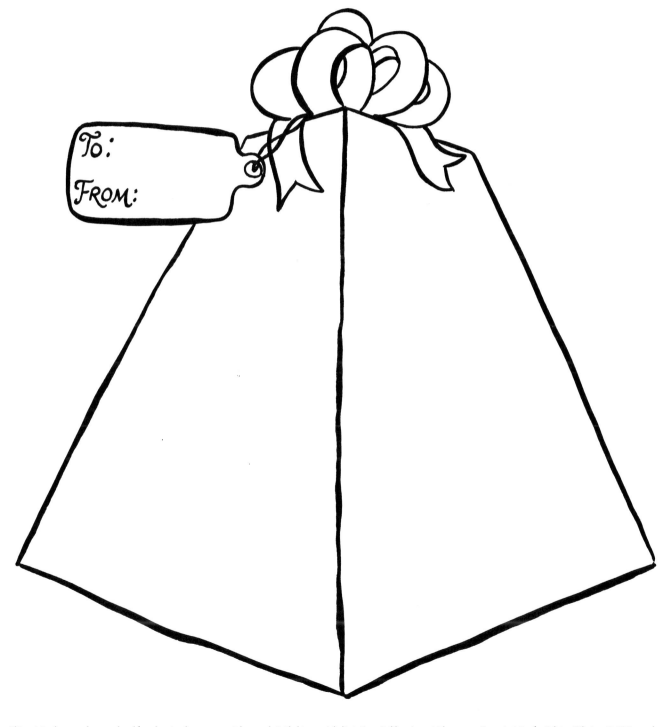

To:

From:

Equality and Social Justice (Asset 27)

Focus
Young participants explore their personal values and beliefs.

Materials
- ☐ Two large signs: one labeled "Agree" and the other "Disagree"
- ☐ Adhesive tape
- ☐ Parents or guardians and other adult participants

Advance Preparations
Invite parents and guardians to participate in this activity. Their presence will help children experience and understand better their values and beliefs.

Compile a list of statements or mottoes that reflect values and beliefs. Be sure to include statements addressing issues of equality and justice that are particularly relevant to the children in your group. Here is a sample list:
- Sticks and stones may break my bones, but words will never hurt me.
- Actions speak louder than words.
- Older kids are mean.
- Younger kids are annoying.
- Anyone can grow up to be the president or leader of this country.
- Poor people work harder than rich people.
- Everybody is born equal.
- A woman's work is never done.
- Experience is the best teacher.
- The best things in life are free.

Tape the large "Agree" sign on one side of the room and the large "Disagree" sign on the opposite side. Clear away any desks or tables to make a space for free movement between the signs.

Activity
In a large group, welcome the adult visitors. Explain that today everyone present will have an opportunity to stand up for what they believe. Explain that you will read a statement and that every person should take a moment to decide whether he or she agrees or disagrees with that statement. Then, people voice their beliefs by standing close to the "Agree" or "Disagree" signs. If they are unsure, they can stand between the signs.

Once people have chosen their spots after the first statement is read, ask a few youth and adult participants to describe the reasons for their choices. Encourage people to move toward the opposite sign if they change their minds after listening to other people's opinions. Stress that being open to revising one's beliefs is a critical characteristic of a thoughtful person. For example, a person who initially agreed that "The best things in life are free" may feel differently after hearing someone else say, "College is not free, and I think an education is the best thing a person can have." A person who initially disagreed may be compelled by the argument, "I think that family is the best thing in life, and you don't have to spend money to belong to a family." Repeat this process for each statement. If time permits, ask group members to suggest other belief statements.

Conclude by conducting a large-group discussion based on the following questions:
- How did you arrive at your original response to each statement?
- Why do we believe what we believe?
- How often did you change your mind when you heard what other people had to say?
- How can we balance our initial "gut" reactions with information we get from other people?
- How do your life experiences influence your beliefs? How do beliefs change as you grow older?

45 — THAT REMINDS ME

Integrity (Asset 28)

Focus
Young people choose objects that help remind them of their core beliefs and values.

Materials
- ☐ Pens or pencils
- ☐ Colored pencils, markers, or crayons
- ☐ Reminder objects to share with the group
- ☐ String or yarn
- ☐ "That Reminds Me" Activity Sheet

Advance Preparations
Assemble a collection of reminder objects to share with the group. Examples might include:
- A red ribbon from Mothers Against Drunk Driving (MADD) reminds me how dangerous it is to ride in a vehicle with a driver who has been drinking alcohol.
- A bumper sticker that reads "Give Peace a Chance" reminds me to resolve my conflicts without violence.
- My book about Martin Luther King Jr. reminds me how important equality is.
- A necklace from my grandmother reminds me to always make time for my family.

Activity
Begin by holding up your finger with the string or yarn tied around it. Ask if anyone knows what this represents. If your group members are unfamiliar with this practice, explain that sometimes a person ties a string around her or his finger as a reminder about something. It is a way to remember to do something or think about something.

Explain that other things can be reminder objects about important beliefs. Hold up each of your reminder objects. Ask the young people to name the object and one belief the object could remind them to think about. Acknowledge that actually living out your beliefs every day can be difficult; sometimes it is helpful to have a symbolic object that is like a string around your finger to remind you to follow your convictions.

Ask for a volunteer to define the word *integrity*. Explain that a person who has integrity doesn't just have strong beliefs, but truly lives her or his life according to those beliefs. Ask for examples of people who have shown integrity. Rosa Parks, an ordinary citizen who did something extraordinary, is one possible example: She not only believed that Black people should have equal rights, but she also took a risk by acting on her beliefs when she refused to give up her seat to a White person on a city bus at a time when Black people were not generally "allowed" to sit in the front of the bus in some cities.

Ask the children to work with partners to discuss the following questions:
- What are some important beliefs that I have?
- How have I acted to show my beliefs?
- What further action can I take to show my beliefs?

Instruct the young people to think of a reminder object that serves one or more of the following purposes:
- The object reminds them of a past action when they showed integrity or acted on their beliefs;
- The object reminds them of a time when someone else showed integrity or acted on their beliefs; or
- The object reminds them to show their beliefs in their present lives.

Distribute the "That Reminds Me" Activity Sheet. Ask participants to draw their reminder objects and to think of one way to turn their belief into an action. During subsequent meetings, invite participants to bring their reminder objects and share them with the group. Encourage kids to share their objects with their family members as well.

That Reminds Me

Sometimes we need help to remind us to act on our beliefs. Think of an object that will remind you to act on a belief that you think is important. Draw a picture of the object.

My reminder object: _____

The belief my reminder object helps me remember:_____
_____

An action I can take based on my belief: _____
_____

INTERNAL ASSETS: POSITIVE VALUES

Honesty (Asset 29)

Focus
Children explore the consequences of dishonesty.

Materials
☐ Pens or pencils
☐ "In Hot Water" Activity Sheet

Activity
Gather the children into a large group. Begin by doing something that is *against* the rules in your school or youth-serving program (for example, eating in the room or drinking a soda). Wait for the children to point out that you're doing something against the rules. Then, hide your food or soda and deny that you were doing anything wrong. The children will likely point out that you are lying. Eventually agree that you are "in hot water." Explain that *being in hot water* is a phrase that means a person is in trouble. Ask: *Why are people tempted to be dishonest when they find themselves in trouble?*

Divide the children into small groups. Ask each group to brainstorm different situations where a young person finds herself or himself "in hot water." Possibilities include a child who hasn't done her or his homework, a child who has broken a valuable object, or a child who has been mean to a sibling.

Ask each group to decide on one situation and to create two scenes to role-play for the larger group, one in which the child "in hot water" lies about her or his situation and the other in which the child decides to come clean and tell the truth. Ask each group to act out their scenes for the larger group. Use the scenes as a springboard for further discussion. Ask:

- How did people around the child react when the child lied? How did they react when the child told the truth?
- Why do people choose to lie? Why do people choose to tell the truth?
- How does it feel inside when you lie? when you tell the truth?

Distribute the "In Hot Water" Activity Sheet along with pens and pencils. Ask the children to work on the sheets in their small groups and share them with one another. End by asking the young people to share statements they can make when they find themselves in hot water but want to tell the truth.

In Hot Water

Sometimes it's hard to tell the truth. In the bathtub below, describe a difficult situation where a young person might feel he or she is "in hot water." In the bubbles, write things a young person could say to be honest and come clean in the situation.

Responsibility (Asset 30)

Focus
Young participants learn to think impartially about taking personal responsibility for their actions.

Materials
- ☐ Children's literature about a character who is reluctant to take responsibility. For example:
  - ➤ *The True Story of the Three Little Pigs* by Jon Scieszka (Viking Children's Books, 1989)
- ☐ Paper
- ☐ Pens or pencils

Advance Preparations
Read your story in advance if you have not already read it. *The True Story of the Three Little Pigs* is a retelling of the classic story from the wolf's point of view. He claims that he was innocent, and simply in the wrong place at the wrong time.

Activity
Read aloud a story about a character who is reluctant to take responsibility for her or his behavior. Invite participants to imagine the story from the defendant's point of view. Ask:
- • What choices did the character make in the story?
- • Do you feel sorry for this character? Why or why not?
- • How is this character blaming others for her or his own mistakes?
- • How might this character take responsibility for her or his actions?

Divide the young people into small groups so that there are enough participants for each character in the story plus one extra person. Have one group member pretend to be a reporter sent from the local paper to interview the characters and investigate what really happened. A group may have multiple reporters if it has extra people. Use these questions to help the reporters:
- • What are the facts in this story?
- • What question could you ask the main character to get her or him to take responsibility for the choices he or she made?
- • How do the other characters feel about the main character's actions?
- • Will you portray the main character as a villain or a victim? Why?
- • What lessons might people learn from this story?

Let participants rotate roles and take turns acting out the various roles. Give them time to write their newspaper accounts. You might conclude the activity with a more reflective discussion that includes these questions:
- • What is hard about taking responsibility for our own actions?
- • What have you learned that will help you take responsibility in your own life?

Optional Variation
Publish the various versions of the story in a homemade newspaper.

Healthy Lifestyle (Asset 31)

Focus
Young people learn that walking is a form of exercise that can help them maintain a healthy lifestyle.

Materials
- ☐ Index cards
- ☐ Pens or pencils
- ☐ Pedometers (optional)
- ☐ "Every Step Counts" Activity Sheet

Activity
Distribute index cards, and begin the activity by asking everyone to walk around the room. Ask young people to silently count their steps and to write that number down on one side of the index card. Next, begin a discussion about exercise:

- How many times a week do you exercise?
- How much time do you spend each time you exercise?
- What activities do you consider exercise?
- What kinds of exercise do you prefer?
- How do you feel before you exercise? after?

If nobody has mentioned it, introduce the idea of walking as exercise. Explain the concept of counting steps and using walking to stay fit. Ask young people to look at the number that they wrote on their index cards. On the reverse side of the card, ask them to record a guess as to how many steps they take in one day.

Distribute the "Every Step Counts" Activity Sheet and invite participants to keep track of their steps. Ask them to record an hour's worth of steps to complete each of the first three items on the sheet. Make plans to calculate the totals next time your group meets.

If you are able to use pedometers, this will simplify the counting process; however, even if young people have trouble keeping track of all of their steps, an estimate is sufficient. Your group's goal should be an increased attention to walking, not a rigid measurement of it.

When the group reconvenes, discuss the following questions:

- Do you think you walked more or fewer steps than the number that you guessed?
- What times of day do you do most of your walking?
- Were there times that you rode in a vehicle when you could have walked?
- What are some simple ways to add steps to your day?

In addition to the ideas that they generate, share these ideas with the group:

- Walk from room to room to speak with family members instead of speaking loudly from the next room.
- Walk around to say "Good morning," "Good afternoon," "Hello," "Good-bye," and "Goodnight" to as many people as possible.
- Use stairs instead of elevators.

Encourage participants to share this information and set walking goals with their families.

Every Step Counts

Try to keep track of your steps for one hour at a time. It can be tricky to count every step, so just do the best you can if you do not have a pedometer that counts the steps for you. Write down how many steps you walk during three different hours in a day. Then use the math calculations below to guess about how many steps you walked in the whole day.

1. Number of steps I walked during one morning hour: _____

2. Number of steps I walked during one afternoon hour: _____

3. Number of steps I walked during one evening hour:_____

4. Adding these three numbers gives a total of _____ steps in three hours.

5. Dividing the total by 3 gives me an average of _____ steps per hour.

6. The time that I woke up on this day: _____

7. The time that I went to bed on this day: _____

8. Total number of hours that I was awake: _____ multiplied by

my average steps per hour from number 5: _____ gives me a

grand total of about _____ steps in one day.

Chapter 9

Social Competencies

Children are impressionable at this age, and they are
learning to interact with many different kinds of people.
These activities help young people develop the skills and
sensitivities they need as they encounter
new friendships and new conflicts.

Planning and Decision Making (Asset 32)

Focus

Young people learn how to break down a large project into smaller steps.

Materials

☐ Paper
☐ Pens or pencils
☐ Index cards
☐ "Step-by-Step Ladder" Activity Sheet

Advance Preparations

Use index cards to prepare task cards for challenging activities that involve several steps. Here are a few possibilities:

- Washing a car;
- Getting ready for bed at night;
- Baking cookies;
- Getting ready for school in the morning;
- Packing a lunch; or
- Planting a garden.

Activity

Divide children into small groups and distribute one task card to each group. Direct each group to divide the task into steps. Instruct each group to write a numbered list of the steps on a piece of paper. Ask each group to share the steps they have identified for their task with the larger group. Encourage them to pantomime the steps.

Point out that almost everything we do in life can be broken down into smaller steps. Even very big projects are made up of smaller steps. We complete any project by completing one step at a time.

Ask the young people to think about a big project, such as cleaning their rooms. Ask them: *Do you ever feel overwhelmed? Do you stand at the doorway of your room and wonder where to begin?* Acknowledge that almost everyone feels overwhelmed when they have a big project they need to complete. Ask:

- What special projects are you always meaning to do that never seem to get done?
- What tasks are you *supposed* to complete that you have trouble finishing?
- When you feel overwhelmed by a big project, what do you do?

Distribute the "Step-by-Step Ladder" Activity Sheet. Invite participants to think through the steps they might take to break down one of their own overwhelming tasks into smaller, more manageable steps. Encourage them to refer back to the activity sheet as they tackle the project.

Optional Variation

Older children who are interested in the steps of community projects might enjoy Search Institute's *Step by Step! A Young Person's Guide to Positive Community Change.* The book is written for ages 13–17, but includes ideas and strategies that would appeal to younger children as well.

Step-by-Step Ladder

The best way to complete a big project is to divide it into smaller steps. Think about a big project you would like to accomplish. Write down the steps you need to take to finish the project on the rungs of the ladder.

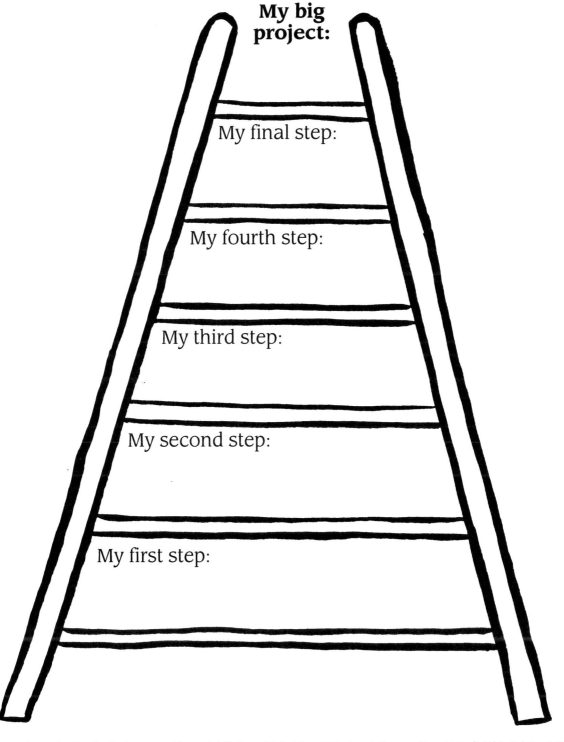

My big project:

My final step:

My fourth step:

My third step:

My second step:

My first step:

Planning and Decision Making (Asset 32)

Focus

Children practice planning and decision-making skills.

Materials

☐ Local and regional maps
☐ Brochures of educational and historical sites
☐ Paper
☐ Pens or pencils
☐ Calculators
☐ Telephones
☐ Library

Activity

Tell the group that they are going to plan a trip together. If possible, let the group plan an actual trip they can take. Be sure to obtain any necessary administrative and parental approval. Possible examples include a visit to a historical site, an overnight trip to an aquarium, or a picnic in a park.

Explain that the group will need to make their plans within a budget. If the group does not already have a budget for this type of activity, calculate a reasonable budget that group members could meet through fund-raising.

Divide the children into small groups to discuss potential locations for the trip. Circulate maps and brochures of sites of possible interest. Ask each group to nominate one location and briefly describe to the larger group why that location might be appealing. Once participants have heard all of the options, ask them to vote on the destination for the trip.

Ask the young people: *What next? How do we get from here to there?* Direct them to identify a list of the areas they will need to plan. Possibilities include:

- Destination hours and fees;
- Transportation;
- Lodging, if staying overnight;
- Food;
- Activities;
- Cost per participant;
- Ideas for fund-raising;
- Chaperones; and
- Permission from parents or guardians.

Assign each small group one or two of the topics. Ask the groups to identify what they need to do to research a particular topic. For example, to plan transportation, the children may need to call the bus company, find out whether parents and guardians are available for carpooling, or talk to a school's transportation coordinator to see if a van is available. Encourage them to research several options in a variety of price ranges.

Have the young people assign each member of their team a task, such as placing a phone call or asking a parent or guardian a question. If necessary, plan a subsequent meeting at a library if the group feels further research will be necessary.

Once the teams have gathered their information, have them present their findings to the larger group. Help the group arrive at decisions that are within the budget. If the most desirable options are overbudget, ask the group where to compromise to lower costs. Ask each team to present at least one less expensive compromise.

Once you have a plan in place, help the group make preparations for the trip. Schedule any necessary fund-raising activities. Once you have attained your monetary goal, invite the young participants to make reservations and other arrangements. Then, take your trip and have fun!

INTERNAL ASSETS: SOCIAL COMPETENCIES

Interpersonal Competence (Asset 33)

Focus
Participants explore how it feels to be included and excluded from a group.

Materials
☐ Large, open space

Activity
Have young people form a circle. Silently survey what they are wearing, and use a clothing type to ask some participants to leave the circle. For example, you might say: *Everyone with a visible number on the outside of her or his clothing should leave the circle.* Other possibilities include shirts with stripes or pants without pockets. Be sure to choose a gender-neutral clothing feature that is not divisive according to economic class, cultural group, or cliques. Avoid using brand names or expensive styles, gang colors, and sports teams to divide the group.

Ask the remaining participants to hold hands. Direct the people outside the circle to take turns trying to push into the circle, but stress that they need to do so in a way that is safe. If someone succeeds in pushing through, he

or she should join the circle and hold hands with the others. Continue until at least two or three people manage to push through into the circle.

Ask everyone to rejoin the group and repeat the activity with a new clothing indicator. However, this time, direct the participants who are outside the circle to simply tap someone on the shoulder to rejoin the circle. That person should release her or his grip and make room for the outsider to join.

Conclude the activity with these questions:
- How did it feel to be part of the circle when you were trying *not* to let people in? Why?
- How did it feel to be outside the circle when people would not let you in? Why?
- How did the second version of the activity feel compared to the first version?
- How were the circles similar to cliques or friendship circles?
- If you want to meet more people and feel comfortable with them, what could you say or do to invite them into your circle? What could you say or do if you want to join a circle of friends?

Interpersonal Competence (Asset 33)

Focus

Children identify good manners that reflect positive self-control.

Materials

☐ Adhesive tape or string
☐ 26 small, blank cards
☐ Pens or pencils
☐ Large, open space for playing the game

Advance Preparations

On each card, write one positive or negative behavior so that you have 13 positive and 13 negative cards. Try to focus on manners and interpersonal skills. Write the description in the first person, past tense.

After each behavior, write a number of steps that coincides with the intensity of the behavior (but do *not* mark the steps as *backward* or *forward*). Very positive or very negative behaviors should have high numbers, and moderately positive or moderately negative behaviors should have low numbers. Here are some examples:

- I talked with my mouth full of food. *Two steps*
- I cleared the table after dinner. *Three steps*
- I had an angry outburst in a restaurant. *Five steps*
- I held the door open for someone. *One step*
- I burped in public without saying, "Excuse me." *One step*
- I told my favorite teacher how much I liked her or his class. *Three steps*
- I cut in front of someone in line. *Three steps*
- I covered my mouth when I coughed. *Two steps*
- I interrupted my parent/teacher/friend while he or she was speaking. *Three steps*

Try to focus on actual behaviors that you have witnessed within your group, but be sure that you are not identifying specific individuals. Shuffle the cards to mix the positive and negative behaviors.

Activity

Begin by asking if anyone knows what a marathon is. Explain that a marathon is a race that is 26 miles long. Announce that you are going to have a manners marathon, but instead of 26 miles, your group will be going through 26 behaviors—13 positive and 13 negative behaviors. Explain that in *this* marathon, some behaviors will actually make you move backward, away from the finish line.

Using tape or string, mark a starting line and a finish line on the ground. Have everyone line up on the starting line. Walk to one end of the line, and ask the first person to draw a card and read it aloud. Ask the participant to identify whether the behavior is positive or negative, and direct her or him to take the number of steps indicated on the card. If the behavior was positive, the person should step forward; if the behavior was negative, he or she should step backward. Be sure to offer guidance if a participant has trouble identifying behaviors accurately.

Walk down the line giving equal turns to all participants. Continue through the cards (reusing them if necessary) until someone crosses the finish line.

When someone crosses the finish line, put her or him in charge of the cards for a new game. Carefully redirect the new leader if he or she has trouble confirming appropriate and inappropriate behaviors.

Optional Variation

Make the game move more quickly by playing in small groups. If you are playing with younger children, modify the steps on the behavior cards to say things like "baby steps," "happy leaps," or "grumpy steps."

Cultural Competence (Asset 34)

Focus

Participants attempt to see the world from someone else's point of view.

Materials

☐ A variety of shoes (enough for one shoe per participant)
☐ Paper
☐ Pens or pencils
☐ Colored pencils, markers, or crayons

Advance Preparations

Collect shoes that might have been worn by people of diverse sizes, ages, and cultures. You could include baby shoes, moccasins, dance slippers, cowboy boots, sandals, or wooden shoes. Each young person will receive only one shoe, so you need not have matching pairs.

Activity

Take your shoes off and hold them up for the group. Ask them to think about the phrase "walking in someone else's shoes." Explore participants' prior knowledge and experiences with empathy by asking:

• How would your life be different if you were walking in my shoes? How would it be the same?
• What does *empathy* mean? What does *compassion* mean?
• What are some examples from your own life of people who show empathy and compassion?

If your group has trouble defining *empathy* and *compassion,* explain that these words refer to people who are kind and are able to understand and respect how other people are feeling. If a person has empathy and compassion, he or she will be thoughtful when imagining "walking in someone else's shoes."

Give each young person one shoe. Invite each participant to picture the person who may have worn her or his shoe. Ask:

• How old would the person be?
• Where might the person live? In which country? In what kind of home?
• What might the person have been doing when he or she was wearing the shoes?
• What are some of the hopes and dreams the person might have had?
• What might be some of that person's challenges?

Encourage the children to try to see the world from that person's point of view. Ask them to avoid negative judgments and to try to respectfully imagine what life is like for the person who once wore that shoe.

Invite them to draw a picture of the person they imagine wearing the shoe. Encourage them to give the person a name, and invite participants to write speeches from the point of view of their imaginary shoe owners. Invite participants to show their pictures and read their speeches aloud.

Optional Variation

For younger participants, suggest that they use the shoes as hand puppets and read their speeches aloud to the group. Afterward let them work in pairs or groups to communicate messages about empathy in puppet shows; the personified shoe characters can interact with each other and show kindness and understanding.

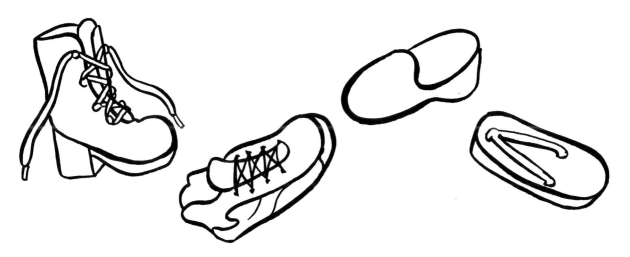

Cultural Competence (Asset 34)

Focus

Participants learn about several different cultures.

Materials

☐ Several different rubber stamps and inkpads

☐ Crayons or markers

☐ Poster board

☐ Scissors

☐ Stapler

☐ Pens or pencils

☐ Sample passport (if available)

☐ Encyclopedias or other library materials about various countries

☐ "Passport Party" Activity Sheet

Advance Preparations

If you do not have a sample passport (or perhaps an expired passport saved as a memento), create one using the "Passport Party" Activity Sheet.

Activity

Begin by explaining that many communities today are made up of people from different parts of the world or of people whose ancestors traveled from across the world. Explain that the group will be doing some "international travel" to explore the cultures that make up their own community.

Break into small groups and ask the young people to discuss the following questions:

• In what country were you born? What about your ancestors?

• Did you or any of your friends, neighbors, or classmates move here from another country? From which countries?

• What is one interesting thing you've learned about another country?

Have each small group identify at least four countries from which they or their ancestors came. Assign one country to each team, and give the teams access to encyclopedias or other library materials so that they can create a small display about the country that the rest of the groups will visit. Encourage them to create posters to welcome travelers to the country, as well as provide information about tourist attractions, the weather, the language, and local customs. They might also draw maps and flags. Ask each group member to practice talking about the country as if he or she were a tour guide.

In a large group, introduce participants to passports, describing their function and features. Ask the children:

• Does anyone have a passport of your own? What country was it issued in?

• Have you traveled abroad and had your passport stamped when entering another country?

• What differences did you notice in comparing the country or countries you were traveling in and where you live now? what similarities?

Circulate a sample passport if you have one available, or pass around the one you have made from the "Passport Party" Activity Sheet. Pass out the "Passport Party" Activity Sheet for participants to fill out. Have them cut out the pages and staple them together to make their passports.

During a subsequent group meeting, have each small group set up a station in the room to represent their country. Invite each group to choose a rubber stamp to use as a passport stamp.

Ask each group to send one member at a time on a visit to the other "countries" and have her or his passport stamped. The other group members should stay at their home station to welcome "travelers," talk about their country, and stamp passports. Encourage the travelers to ask questions about the different countries. Rotate responsibilities until each child has had an opportunity to visit each "country."

Optional Variation

Invite kids to draw currency, offer ethnic food, and sell products, such as homemade postcards or jewelry made out of pasta and string.

Passport Party

To visit other countries, you need a passport. Draw a picture of yourself and fill in the blanks to create your passport and become a world traveler. You can cut out the pages below and staple them together into a passport of your own. Every time you visit a "country," make sure to get your passport stamped!

MY PASSPORT

My Picture

Full Name: _____

_____

Date of Birth: _____

Citizenship: _____

Places I've Visited

Resistance Skills (Asset 35)

Focus

Children name strategies for resisting negative peer pressure.

Materials

☐ Pens or pencils

☐ "Wolf Pack Power" Activity Sheet

Activity

Talk a little bit about wolves. Explain that they travel in a pack, working together to survive in the wilderness and protect one another. Ask the children what other groups or "packs" travel together and look out for one another. Examples might include families, sports teams, or kids in classrooms. Ask the kids:

- What packs of kids spend time with you?
- How do the kids in your pack look out for you? How do they keep you away from danger?
- How might you resist if the kids in your pack tempted you to do something you shouldn't do?

Divide the children into small groups. Invite them to list the places that young people interact, such as the classroom, cafeteria, bus, hallways, playground, shopping malls, neighborhood parks, and recreation centers. Ask

them to choose one setting and think of a situation where a group of kids might pressure another kid to do something bad. For example, kids hanging out at the shopping mall might pressure another kid to shoplift or steal.

Invite the children to role-play a scene in the situation that they have chosen. Ask one child to play the role of a person who is trying to pressure someone into a negative behavior, and ask a second child to be the person who tries to resist the pressure. Invite several other volunteers to be the wolf pack. Ask them to first help apply negative pressure. Halfway through the role play, ask the pack to help the pressured kid resist the negative behavior. Conclude with these questions:

- What kinds of things do kids say to get other kids to do bad things?
- What can a kid say to resist negative pressure from other kids?
- What positive things can kids say or do to help another kid when he or she is being pressured?

Distribute the "Wolf Pack Power" Activity Sheet. Invite participants to identify the positive friends in their own "wolf pack" who help them make good choices. Ask them to write dialogue that their group members might use to help them resist negative peer pressure.

Wolf Pack Power

Are there kids in your "pack" or who you'd like to have in your "pack" who look out for you? On each wolf below, write the name of one kid who helps you resist negative pressure from other kids. What are some of the things each of your friends say to help you make safe, smart choices? Write those words in that wolf's "speaking balloon."

Peaceful Conflict Resolution (Asset 36)

Focus
Young people identify positive conflict resolution strategies.

Materials
- ☐ Glue
- ☐ Highlighter
- ☐ Eraser
- ☐ Scissors
- ☐ Calculator
- ☐ Paper
- ☐ Crayons, markers, or colored pencils

Activity
Display the materials listed and introduce the activity with this speech:

> *Welcome to the Work-It-Out Shop. This is the place where people shop for tools they can use to solve problems in positive ways. Come inside for a tour.*

Ask the young people to predict how these objects would help someone fix a problem. Act as a tour guide and introduce each displayed item using the following ideas:

- Glue: *Stick with it. If your first solution doesn't work, try another.*
- Highlighter: *Highlight the problem, not the person.*
- Eraser: *Erase blame and take responsibility for the choices you made in the situation.*
- Scissors: *Cut to the truth.*
- Calculator: *Calculate win-win solutions. Keep things equal, and don't be divided.*

Ask participants: *What other tools might you find in the Work-It-Out Shop?* Invite them to draw or invent tools that would help them reach peaceful solutions. Invite them to add their tool to the collection and describe how they would use it to work through conflicts.

Ask each child to choose one tool and think of a specific situation where using that tool could lead to a peaceful solution to the conflict. For example: *When would erasing blame with an eraser be helpful?*

Invite the kids to make radio announcements to advertise their tools. Suggest that they include testimonials about how well the tool worked in a specific situation.

INTERNAL ASSETS: SOCIAL COMPETENCIES

Positive Identity

Children often struggle to develop a sense of control
and purpose. The activities in this chapter allow
young people to explore their identities and
feel positive about their roles in the world.

Personal Power (Asset 37)

Focus
Participants identify choices that are within their control.

Materials
☐ Sample remote control
☐ Cardboard
☐ Large beads or buttons
☐ Glue
☐ Markers

Activity
Gather the young people in a large group and introduce this activity by holding up a TV remote control. Pretend that you've never seen one before. Ask:
- What's this thing called?
- So what does it do?
- What do all these different buttons do?

Then say: *That's a pretty cool thing, but too bad all it does is control your TV. Wouldn't it be neat if we had remote controls to turn on our own personal power source?* Ask the children how such a remote control might function. To spark their thinking, ask:
- How do you "turn on" personal power?
- Which personal power skills might the "pause" button represent?
- Which button might represent listening skills?
- How would you use your volume buttons in real life?
- When does it feel like your remote control is broken? What can you do then?

As the young people brainstorm about what personal power choices might appear on their remote control, challenge them to think creatively about how to make positive decisions. Invite the young participants to create a large three-dimensional model of their own personal power remote control. Ask them to label the different buttons so others can understand their functions. Invite each to share her or his invention with the large group and describe its features.

Optional Variation
Invite participants to create remote controls as gifts to younger children to teach them about personal power.

INTERNAL ASSETS: POSITIVE IDENTITY

Self-Esteem (Asset 38)

Focus
Children identify and celebrate their own talents, skills, and achievements.

Materials
- [ ] Paper
- [ ] Pens or pencils
- [ ] Permanent or acrylic markers or fabric paint
- [ ] Scrap fabric, old sheets, or a T-shirt

Advance Preparations
Construct a simple cape for yourself out of fabric.

Activity
Begin a large-group discussion while wearing your cape. Explain that you are wearing the cape because you are celebrating your "cape-abilities." Describe a modest challenge you were able to meet or obstacle that you were able to overcome recently, such as balancing your checkbook or finally cleaning out your refrigerator. Identify the super powers that helped you succeed, such as your mathematical brain or your superhuman cleaning abilities. Say: *I'm really feeling good about myself and proud of who I am.*

Invite young people to share their thoughts about superheroes. Ask them:
- What are the names of some of your favorite superheroes?
- What kinds of powers do those superheroes have?
- How did those superheroes use their powers to overcome problems?

Suggest that although we might not feel like we have dramatic adventures quite like a superhero, every person has super strengths to celebrate.

Invite young people to talk in pairs and share with their partners situations in which they conquered a challenge using their own strengths and talents. If they have trouble identifying challenging situations, you might use these questions to generate ideas:
- How did you feel when you read your first chapter book cover to cover?
- How did it feel when you helped your parent or guardian make pancakes or scrambled eggs for the first time?
- How do you feel when you solve a difficult math problem by yourself?
- How do you feel when you complete an especially long bike ride?

Invite the pairs of kids to celebrate their successes by designing capes that showcase their talents and achievements. Encourage them to write slogans or sayings that reflect their personal abilities, such as "Brilliant Basketball Player" or "Super Smart Student."

Optional Variation
Arrange for older children to interview kids in 1st or 2nd grade to find out about their talents, skills, and achievements. The older children can design capes for their younger "superheroes" and plan a celebration to encourage their new friends to keep striving for success. Celebrate younger children's super powers by having them wear their capes and create dramatic reenactments of their accomplishments.

Sense of Purpose (Asset 39)

Focus

Children investigate jobs that interest them and contact someone in their chosen field to explore how a job can give someone a sense of purpose.

Materials

☐ Pens or pencils

☐ Paper

☐ Envelopes

☐ Postage

☐ Internet to access information about careers and vocations. Visit the:

➤ Bureau of Labor Statistics' kid-friendly site that's easy to navigate at www.bls.gov/k12/html/edu_over.htm

☐ Library: Many have a "vocations" drawer filled with pamphlets on a wide variety of careers ranging from pet groomers to genetic counselors. Each booklet typically includes addresses and Web sites for further information. Two series include:

➤ *Occupational Briefs* by Chronicle Guidance Publications, Inc.

➤ *Careers Research Monographs* by the Institute for Research Chicago

☐ "A Job to Enjoy" Activity Sheet

Advance Preparations

Visit the library or Web sites to obtain books and pamphlets and other information on various careers.

Activity

Begin a large-group discussion by asking the young people: *Why is having a job so important?* Acknowledge that financial realities require that most people work. But probe further to discuss how people's work relates to their sense of purpose. Many people feel their work is helping others or somehow making the world a better place. Other people gain a sense of purpose from working as a team with their coworkers and finishing tasks together.

Share the books and pamphlets and other career information you collected from the library and Web sites. Invite the young participants to look at them and consider jobs they might like to hold as adults. Ask them to list all the possibilities on a sheet of paper. Then, ask them to identify one occupation in particular that intrigues them. Ask them to consider how that job might give them a sense of purpose.

Distribute the "A Job to Enjoy" Activity Sheet to help the young people think further about the job that most interests them. Give participants some time to fill in the first few blanks. Then, using the career information gathered, or gather more if necessary, ask the children to try to fill in the rest of the blanks, but assure them that leaving blanks is fine if they are unsure of an answer.

Using the activity sheet as a starting point and contact information from the career pamphlets and booklets, invite participants to write letters to people working in their fields of interest to learn more about the career. Give children a letter template to use as a guide. In their letters, the children can explain why they are interested in the job and what they already know about the field. Then, they can request that the recipients write back and answer questions about the daily duties of the job, special challenges and rewards, as well as how the job contributes to their sense of purpose.

Review each letter before mailing. Use your program's or school's return address to avoid sharing private addresses with unfamiliar adults. When young people receive responses, invite them to share their letters with the group.

A Job to Enjoy

Fill in the blanks below to explore a job that interests you. Fill in numbers 1 and 2 first. Then stop and do some research before filling in the remaining items.

1. One job that interests me is: _____

_____.

2. What I already know about this job: _____

_____.

3. The education or training for this job includes: _____

_____.

4. Some daily duties of this job are: _____

_____.

5. A challenge of this job would be: _____

_____.

6. The best part of this job would be: _____

_____.

7. I would gain a sense of purpose from this job because: _____

_____.

60 — NAME POEMS

Sense of Purpose (Asset 39)

Focus
Young people identify how they might use their talents, skills, and interests to make the world a better place for themselves and others.

Materials
- ☐ Paper
- ☐ Crayons, markers, and colored pencils

Advance Preparations
Write a biographical poem in which each letter of your name begins a phrase that describes one of your qualities, as in this poem using the name Ruth:

> **R**uth is my name.
> **U**nderstanding is my game.
> **T**eaching is very important to me.
> **H**elping others makes me happy.

Activity
Read your biographical poem and share with the children a little bit about your own life story. Explain how you found your life's purpose: What sparked your interest in working with children? Talk about the people who inspired you to use your talents and skills to help others.

Explain to participants that the name poem is one way to celebrate a sense of purpose in life. You could mention that famous writers William Shakespeare and Lewis Carroll inserted special names in the beginning lines of their poems; the composer Johann Sebastian Bach included his name represented by certain notes in his musical compositions, too!

Invite young people to create autobiographical "Name Poems." Explain that rhyming is not necessary. Use these questions to help them generate ideas for writing:

- What are some qualities that describe who you are as a person?
- What are your talents and skills?
- What are some of the good things that you do for other people?

Give participants time to write their poems, and encourage them to draw illustrations if they like. Have a poetry reading in which volunteers read their poems to the rest of the group.

61 — MIRROR IMAGE

Positive View of Personal Future (Asset 40)

Focus
Participants explore optimistic visions of their futures.

Materials
- ☐ Several mirrors
- ☐ Paper
- ☐ Pens or pencils
- ☐ Colored pencils, markers, or crayons
- ☐ "Mirror Image" Activity Sheet

Activity
Pass around mirrors and ask that every young person take a careful look at her or his reflection. When all group members have had a chance to look in a mirror, ask them to spend a few minutes writing quietly in response to these questions:

- What do you see when you look in the mirror?
- What important parts of your personality are not visible?
- What kind of person would you want to look back at you from the mirror next year?
- How would you make that person happen?
- In what ways would you like to grow and change by next summer?
- How will you change during the next school year?

Pass out the "Mirror Image" Activity Sheet. Ask the children to draw pictures of the important things they see themselves doing next year. Invite the children to share their drawings with the larger group. Ask them: *What do you think will be the same about yourselves this time next year? What will be different?*

INTERNAL ASSETS: POSITIVE IDENTITY

Mirror Image

Draw a picture of the important things you see yourself doing in the next year.

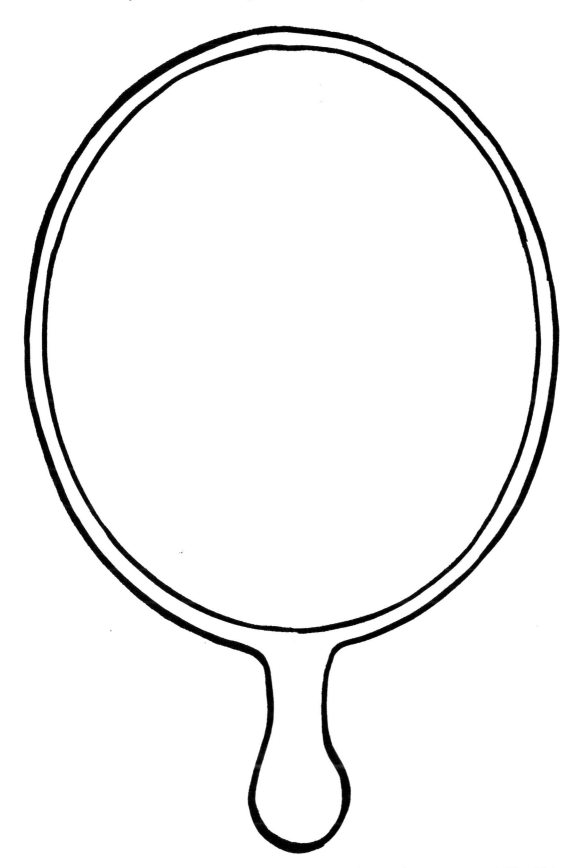

Other Resources from Search Institute

150 Ways to Show Kids You Care

Many adults want to strengthen their relationships with kids—they just don't know how. Use this attractive mini-poster as a handout to inspire and motivate adults with practical ideas for showing kids they care. Distribute it to parents, teachers, youth workers, congregations, and community residents.

Ideas for Parents CD-ROM

Packed with the information parents need, these 52 newsletters are the perfect outreach tool. The CD also includes a user's guide with suggestions for customizing and distributing the series.

Great Group Games
175 Boredom-Busting, Zero-Prep Team Builders for All Ages

This best-selling book offers 175 enjoyable games and activities that are perfect for classrooms, retreats, workshops, and groups on the go. Each game includes details on timing, supplies, setup, suggested group size, game tips, and reflection questions. Far from mindless time wasters, these games offer fun and meaningful options for every group.

Raising Kids with Care
50 Ways to Help Your Whole Family Thrive

Use this list of comforting, practical tips and reminders to build assets for your children *and* take care of yourself. Filled with thoughtful insights and realistic reminders in both English and Spanish, it offers a much-needed boost to parents.

Pass It On at School!
Activity Handouts for Creating Caring Schools

Schools where students feel valued, supported, and cared for are the best places to learn. These ready-to-use tip sheets and handouts, based on the 40 Developmental Assets, equip everyone in the school community to create change for the better.

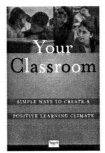

Your Classroom
Simple Ways to Create a Positive Learning Climate

This introduction to Developmental Assets is loaded with easy ways teachers can build relationships with young people, create a positive classroom environment, and infuse assets into their existing practices. Sold in packs of 20 so every teacher in your school can have one handy.

Coming into Their Own
How Developmental Assets Promote Positive Growth in Middle Childhood

Children in middle childhood are approaching the cusp of early adolescence and beginning the transition to selfhood and self-regulation. This book the research to help parents and other adults understand what is most effective and helpful to kids during this critical stage of development.

Parenting Preteens with a Purpose

This nurturing, research-based guide offers tips, checklists, and solutions to common parenting topics, including preteen friendships, clothes and hair preferences, after-school hours, crushes, and finding a work-home balance. Sympathetic, respectful, and grounded in the Developmental Assets, this handbook provides abundant "on-the-job" support to parents.